Praise for Raised Healthy, Wealthy & Wise

"Move over, Spock and Brazelton! You'll want to make room on your bookshelf for this down-to-earth guide for parents who may live on Easy Street, but still struggle to know what's best for their children. Her stories about inheritors present teachable moments and ring very true indeed."

—Charlotte Beyer, Founder, Institute for Private Investors;
President, Principle Quest Foundation

"What makes this book unique and valuable is that the stories of real-life successful inheritors found here resonate, particularly their surprising insights about accountability, independence, and being able to feel that they earned their own successes. Wealthy parents seeking advice on how to raise their children well amid wealth will find in these words the inspiration and conviction needed for them to implement these best practices in their own families."

—Sara Hamilton, Founder and CEO, Family Office Exchange

"*Raised Healthy, Wealthy & Wise* is a breath of fresh air in the discussion about how inheritors can prosper with wealth. Compared to the countless books and articles emphasizing how debilitating wealth is, Covie Edwards-Pitt has taken the unique approach of interviewing successful, strong heirs to discover what may have contributed to their success as adults. She sifts through their stories to uncover nuggets of wisdom about the essential contribution of strong parental role-models, early paid work, core values, and high standards in forging personalities capable of harnessing the power of affluence. Like other recent books on wealth emphasizing a positive-psychology approach, *Raised Healthy,*

D1110247

Wealthy & Wise offers parents more advice about 'how-to' than 'how-not-to.' It is a welcome addition to the field."

>—*James Grubman, Ph.D., Principal, FamilyWealth*
>*Consulting; wealth psychologist and author of* Strangers
>in Paradise: How Families Adapt to Wealth Across
>Generations

"*Raised Healthy, Wealthy & Wise* is a must read for wealthy parents who want to ensure their children's health, happiness and engagement in life. The book's extensive research is a major contribution to our field."

>—*Ryan Ansin, President, Family Office Association;*
>*Co-Founder, Clarity Project*

"An insider's view of a neglected but important topic, *Raised Healthy, Wealthy & Wise: Lessons from Successful Inheritors on How They Got That Way* is a valuable addition to the literature on avoiding the perils of privilege."

>—*Wendy Mogel, Ph.D., author of* The Blessing of a Skinned
>Knee *and* The Blessing of a B Minus

". . . an important book that offers a refreshing perspective on the subject of raising children amid great wealth. It is rare to find research based on the experiences of inheritors who have found their paths to personal fulfillment and to hear in their own voices what they believe led to their successes."

>—*Sharna Goldseker, Executive Director, 21/64*

"If you were raised wealthy but NOT healthy and wise, then you'll find yourself nodding at the description of challenges you're facing, and feel empowered by the success stories outlined in this book. Your road will not be easy (I doubt it is for anybody), but you will not find a better source of real stories and real advice from people who have walked in your shoes, curated by an advisor with real experience in the challenges of inherited wealth. If you're a wealthy parent, these success stories offer a road map for giving your own children the gift of a meaningful life outside the deep, potentially debilitating shadows of inheritance."

—*Bob Veres, Editor,* Inside Information

"The author has given readers a lot to consider. She asks, and through her careful and thoughtful research is able to answer, the question of what parents of successful inheritors have done. We have been waiting for a book like this for a long time."

—*Angelo Robles, Founder and CEO, Family Office Association*

"For most families, more money means less stress. But for those who've accumulated the kind of wealth that can land you in the pages of *Forbes* magazine, the American dream can quickly become a nightmare of bad parenting and unhealthy financial consequences. Ms. Edwards-Pitt's new book goes beyond the typical financial advice book and instead gets its practical strategies from real-life rich kids who have grown up into balanced, confident and productive adults."

—*Matt Schifrin, Managing Editor,* Forbes

RAISED HEALTHY, WEALTHY & WISE

Raised Healthy, Wealthy & Wise

Lessons from successful and grounded inheritors on how they got that way

Coventry Edwards-Pitt

Contents

Acknowledgments

A heartfelt thank you to:

The interviewees—I am grateful for your willingness to open your hearts and share your experiences so candidly with me. I have learned so much from your stories and trust many others will be inspired by them.

Our clients—I can't imagine a more fulfilling career than being given the opportunity to help you solve problems and achieve your goals. Thank you for allowing me to share the ups and downs of your lives, see your dreams come to fruition, and watch your children grow.

My partners and professional colleagues—It's a joy coming to work and serving families with you. A special thank you to Roy Ballentine for his mentorship over the years and to Roy Ballentine, Drew McMorrow, and the rest of my partners for believing in the importance of this work and enabling me to dedicate the time to its creation: Lorne Adrain, Karen Anthony, Nicole Bailey, Katerina Barka, Liz Biddle, Will Braman, Tom Bullitt, Carol Chamberlain, Michael Chimento, Lisa Cunningham,

Taryn Dawson, Jayson DeAngelis, Andrea Dubuc, Brie Elliott, Kim Emberg, Nick Ferbert, Jackie Finneron, Ann Fisher, Elaine Gillim, Sam Gough, Michelle Harrison, Naz Hassanein, Danielle Hatch, Alexander Knapp, Aaron Laufer, Sheila Lawrence, Aaron MacDougall, Steve Martone, Kim Maxfield, Edie Miller, Sam Nofzinger, Adam Ochlis, Paul Olzerowicz, Peter Peng, Greg Peterson, Jeanne Pochily, Austin Poirier, Jeff Potter, Valerie Pycko, Derek Roberge, Kyle Schaffer, Claudia Shilo, Susan Stevens, Shannon Tibbetts, Will Tickle, Barry Tubman, Leah Warren, Stephanie Weitzman, Natascha Whelan, Debra Whitney, Morgan Williams, Julia Zhu.

The great minds in our field whose work and thought leadership informed both this book and our practice. A special thank you to Dr. James Grubman, Ph.D., whose 10-year relationship with our firm and thoughtful monthly trainings have immeasurably deepened my understanding of the psychology of wealth: Charlotte Beyer, Barbara Blouin, Fredda Herz Brown, Scott Budge, Charlie Collier, Christopher and Anne Ellinger, Scott Fithian, Jason Franklin, Eileen and Jon Gallo, Kelin Gersick, Joline Godfrey, Sharna Goldseker, Sara Hamilton, Lee Hausner, Cheryl Holland, Jay Hughes, Dennis Jaffe, Ivan Lansberg, Ross Levin, John Levy, Charles Lowenhaupt, Kathryn McCarthy, Stephen McCarthy, Arden O'Connor, Victor Preisser, Abby Raphel, Joe Reilly, Angelo Robles, Greg Rogers, Tom Rogerson, Myra Salzer, Paul Schervish, Bob Veres, John A. Warnick, Keith Whitaker, Roy Williams, Thayer Willis.

Katrin Schumann—Thank you for your insights, good humor, and belief in this topic. Your work helping me to define and shape the project and find the right words was invaluable.

Janie Doherty—Thank you for your herculean efforts scheduling countless interviews, managing the book production calendar, and tracking down out-of-print publications and obscure references. I truly could not have done this project without your steady assistance day in and day out!

The book production team—Thank you to Kimberley Emberg for managing the publication process, David Wilk for everything from big-picture cheerleading to nuts-and-bolts shepherding of copyediting, typesetting, and printing, Alexander Duckworth, Elijah Duckworth-Schachter, Kate Dell'Aquila, and Katie Jansen from Point One Percent for their beautiful cover design, and Peter Haines for believing in this project and helping to get it off the ground.

My family—Thank you to my mother for all you did to help me launch independently and confidently into life. To my father whose sense of humor and love of learning have always been an inspiration to me. And to my brother and his wife, thank you for being there to laugh with and for being such wonderful role models for my daughter.

My husband—Thank you for being a true partner in life and for making it fun.

My daughter—Thank you for showing me every day that the joys of parenting far outweigh the challenges.

Raised Healthy, Wealthy & Wise

Introduction

When new clients come to us for advice, they often believe their biggest challenge is whether or not they will achieve investment returns that will both preserve and grow their wealth. But, if they have children, it's likely their biggest problem lies elsewhere—and that it is, in many ways, more intractable: It is whether their wealth will interfere with their children's ability to launch successful and independent lives.

This challenge is the hardest to address because of two simple facts. First, while money usually helps solve problems, in this case money actually exacerbates them. Second, much of the work to fix this problem must be done by the parents themselves, and the earlier the better. This is why we are writing this book: to inspire readers to do the hard work of communicating certain important messages to their children and to give them a road map to show them how. By sharing the stories of adult children who have absorbed and put into play these messages and are now living productive and engaged lives, we will illustrate how critical it is that wealthy parents take the reins rather than assuming that everything will work itself out.

Families with great wealth have great complications to deal with. Their lives can be enviable, but their lives are also invariably filled with unique psychological stresses brought on by their wealth. In our industry we regularly encounter inheritors, whether they are first, second, or third generation, whose relationship with money is so complicated and conflicted that it becomes the single problem that defines their lives. When they're faced with the inevitable complications that intergenerational money transfer causes, they are dealing with topics that for them are intensely private, delicate, and, often, confounding. They struggle with conflicting emotions and a sense of futility for which there is often no easy solution.

Why is it that some children born to wealth develop into successful, grounded adults and yet others do just the opposite? What did the parents of successful inheritors do—or what did they *not* do—that resulted in individuals who found paths to genuine personal fulfillment rather than being corrupted or distracted by their easy access to money? What are the lessons other parents and inheritors can learn from the positive experiences of these inheritors, so they can avoid the pitfalls that wealthy children so often stumble into, sometimes with catastrophic results?

Asking the courageous questions

The wealthy families who seek our help handling their finances are sophisticated and outcome oriented. The initial needs they have identified are concrete and practical: They want help protecting their wealth, finding investment opportunities, identifying risks, and avoiding mistakes. These are what I call their *basic needs*: nuts-and-bolts advice and implementation. It's the main reason they come to wealth management firms like ours.

But what they learn is that these are actually the easy issues to deal with. There are clear solutions and we can find them. The much harder issue to address—and where we therefore spend a lot of time with clients—is navigating the complex interaction between wealth and child rearing. How do I make sure this money has a positive, not negative, impact on my children? Will my giving money to my child make it easier or harder for them to be successful on their own? And, if my child is struggling, is this the short-term pain that is necessary for the long-term gain?

These are the types of deep questions that we prompt our clients to contemplate. While our conversations touch on broader themes of values and legacy, they continually come back to the issue of the children. All the money in the world is meaningless if you are worried about your child's health, happiness, or engagement in life. It is all the more tragic if it's actually the money itself that is compounding the child's problems and heightening your concerns.

Ironically, at a certain level of wealth, money makes parenting harder, not easier. In his new book, *David and Goliath*, Malcolm Gladwell discusses this phenomenon with Dr. James Grubman, using the concept of an inverted U-curve to explain that money makes parenting easier up to a certain income level, at which point it begins to make it harder.[1] This means that to have the same chance of raising a well-launched child, parents with wealth have to work harder than parents who are less wealthy. They have to be proactive, consistent, and engaged when it's all too easy and tempting to be just the opposite. Wealthy parents often make the mistake of thinking that the only education they need to provide as a result of their money is about the money itself. The reality is that the mere presence of wealth amplifies the consequences of normal parenting interactions, which, on the surface, may have nothing at all to do with money.

We have all seen the consequences when this goes badly. As wealth advisors, we are often asked to help address difficulties with now grown children. The sad reality is that, while our advice is urgently needed in these situations, much of what we spend our time on is minimizing the downside, either establishing parameters that stem the outflow of dissipated inheritance or desperately trying to reorient the child toward a vocation they may find fulfilling and lasting. We can do much to improve the outcome in these cases, but it's very difficult to match the outcome that might have existed if the child had been exposed earlier to the values and lessons that would have enabled them to launch successfully and independently into life.

While there is a lot of advice out there for affluent parents, no one has focused exclusively on success stories—children who survived the gauntlet of being raised with wealth and emerged happy, healthy, and productive on the other side. Our goal was to hear from them: Why do they think they have become successful? What went right? And how? Our hope is that these voices from the future will speak louder than a litany of advice books and will inspire parents currently faced with these challenges to take the steps necessary now to set their children on the path toward health and happiness.

A coaching role

As a child, I always wanted to become a doctor. From an early age onwards I was driven by a desire to help people, and I found myself in the wealth management industry for the same reason many others gravitate toward this field: We are service oriented. It is immensely rewarding to do work that results in tangible benefits—emotionally as well as financially—for our clients.

Our field is evolving rapidly, and being at the forefront of this groundswell allows us to do meaningful work that has real impact. We have consistently found that the more we provide a holistic service model, the better results we see. On occasion, people refer to us jokingly as financial therapists, but in reality we are more like coaches: We listen to our clients' concerns, giving them both the time and the opportunity to delve deeply into issues, and then offer practical advice for ways to address them.

Ultimately, we really are seeking to help our clients not just manage their wealth, but improve their lives by finding a better synergy between their values and their money. Nowhere is this synergy more important than in child rearing. This "coaching" puts us in a unique position to recognize problems that parents often underestimate or even deny. In offering them the space and time to talk though intimate conflicts and emotions around money, we frequently encounter an inability to identify, accept, and change problems relating to their children.

Every parent, regardless of their income level, hopes their children will launch into adult life with confidence and full of potential. But it is not enough to hope, especially when money is involved. Over the years, we have found that it is often the wealth itself that stands in the way.

We've all known distraught parents who live enviable lives with plenty of money whose children are resentful and unhappy and struggle to make their own way in the world. These are grown children who remain childlike far too long: They are dependent, judgmental, bitter, unfocused, and, often, misguided. They suffer from depression, boredom, and alienation. Many just stumble along making it up as they go along, carrying with them a mysterious combination of resentment and guilt. What is especially tragic is that even though they desperately want to lead meaningful lives, these young people are often paralyzed by a sense of futility and anger.

The irony is that in spite of having plenty of money, these inheritors feel cheated. And as crazy as it may sound, they have in fact been cheated: of the opportunity to live a life fueled by a sense of personal accomplishment and drive. It is heartbreaking because it is avoidable—but not without hard work.

The parents of these frustrated inheritors often have no idea what they have done wrong. Their intentions were good, but their execution was flawed. They are perplexed and exasperated by their children, while knowing deep down that it's not really their children who are to blame.

The hard work of parenting

Raising children is surely one of the most satisfying, maddening, and effortful labors any individual can undertake. There are no panaceas and no guarantees. And what no advisor can do—and no book can take on—is the hard work of parenting itself. Even the best intentioned, seasoned, and patient advisor will not be able to correct for years of poor parenting or replace the need for parents to teach these lessons consistently and clearly over the years. This is true regardless of whether you enjoy great wealth or not.

Over the years, we have encountered many families who get it right. Their children grow into responsible, grateful, purposeful, independent adults. They share healthy and loving relationship with their parents, and find ways to define themselves independently.

How, we began to wonder, to account for this variability of outcomes? Why, on the one hand, do some children grow up in wealth and turn that to their advantage, enjoying a sense of meaning and connection, while, for others, the wealth seems to be an albatross denying them self-worth and a purposeful daily existence?

Over time, we saw patterns emerging. We realized that the families with the most successful children—young adults who are financially and emotionally independent of their parents—were conveying similar core messages to their children. Wanting to know more, I began conducting interviews and delved deeply and relentlessly into questions about work, self-esteem, independence, purpose, and judgment. This book examines those messages and shows how they help create exactly the kind of structure and sense of purpose that money can take away.

In the chapters ahead, we look at what it really means to have "successful" children and describe the parenting behavior that best promotes this kind of bedrock success. We hear about parents biting the bullet and enforcing limits with their children and holding them accountable for their mistakes. We hear how rewarding striving to succeed is a critical but challenging goal for parents when money can so easily buy success. We see messages of financial and emotional independence reflected in stories about waitressing, parking cars, and paying bills in college, and we are continually reminded that children are proudest of themselves when they feel they have achieved their success on their own. We analyze whether openness about inheritance creates opportunity or seeds lethargy. And as we predicted, we see that work—whether mundane or impassioned—is the key to a sense of purpose and freedom.

The personal stories these successful inheritors shared with us highlight that parents must not only be intentional and consistent in conveying these core messages, but must walk the walk themselves. In every interview, I hear the love and respect grown children feel for parents who made the time to be engaged and authentic role models. After dozens of interviews, I have gathered insights that will inform my continuing work with our clients and their families, and have been reminded of the powerful role we can play in helping them shape contented lives for themselves and their children.

Parents have a golden moment when their children are young, which they must seize—or risk having to endure years of stress, worrying about their child's failure to launch. Nothing is more powerful than showing children, from an early age onwards, what financial literacy really looks like in action. You can tell a child how important it is to work, to spend sensibly, to think ahead, to connect with others, to live within their means. But nothing teaches them more effectively than giving them the opportunity to experience these realities on their own, over time—to demonstrate for themselves that they are able to handle "real life."

How this book works

There are many nuts-and-bolts advice books on raising children in affluence, aimed at parents doing their best to raise happy, independent children who have not been demotivated or disempowered by their wealth. But these books differ from ours in two important ways: First, ours focuses on success stories, and second, we hear directly from real inheritors, now grown, and learn what they think contributed to their success.

We hear so much doom and gloom, and yet we do not hear much from the younger generation who internalized important messages growing up and then put those messages into practice, to good effect, through the daily choices they make about work, love, and civic engagement. Where are the stories about children of wealth who have grown up balanced and confident: "successful"? This book focuses on these young people instead of their parents, giving strategic advice that is grounded more in demonstrable realities than in abstractions.

Also, while the wealth management industry is replete with solid next-generation education, starting at that point is late in the game. It's like arming a child with scuba equipment before he or she has learned to swim. Working with a financial literacy advisor is certainly valuable for individuals who find themselves lost in the adult world of planning, saving, and spending. But to enter adulthood with your best foot forward, nothing is as effective as learning these fundamental lessons early, often, and in the home. Research shows that for parents to really set their children on the right path, the focus should be on teaching the right values and providing opportunities to absorb these lessons.

We have studied new research on child development to see how it relates to the unique and poorly understood difficulties that affluent children experience. In the past few years alone, new findings in brain science, psychology, and happiness research have led to a slew of important books on child development, motivation, workplace realities, and individual potential. While we promote using these invaluable resources, the truth is that real life too often gets in the way. Our clients don't have time to read ten books and untangle the ways these lessons relate to their own lives as first-, second-, or third-generation inheritors. The most germane nuggets from these thought leaders inform each chapter, allowing you to access the latest information without having to do all the research yourself.

In writing this book, we decided to focus on interviewing inheritors whom we consider to be successful (more on how we define that in the next chapter). Over the course of some months, I conducted dozens of interviews that ran about two hours. When a family had multiple children, I strove to interview each of the siblings, asking the identical questions and gauging the consistency of the messages and values conveyed.

Each time, the same pattern emerged: At the start, both the interviewee and I would wonder whether my 15-question interview list would really produce enough discussion to last for the full 120 minutes we had scheduled. But we would invariably find ourselves deeply immersed in private and often emotional conversations that went to the very core of how the interviewee defined themselves and their position in the world.

Oftentimes, our conversations took us totally by surprise—leading to epiphanies and resolutions. More than once I was told that the questions conjured up forgotten and powerful memories. Several people asked for recordings of their interviews to share with family members and children. There were often tears. I was as enlightened and enriched by the experience as my interviewees. Sharing in their private recollections and helping them untangle the messages they received and the impact these messages had on them was an honor.

For the first time the lens was focused on the inheritors themselves, and while we also looked at their struggles, we analyzed most closely the root causes of their successes. In this book we aim to answer the question: "What actually encourages a child of a wealthy family to achieve success on his or her own?" In so doing, we hope to put the advice contained in myriad other books in the industry through the test of real-life circumstance.

A note about privacy

Talking about money makes most people uncomfortable. How much money you make, save, and spend is a highly private concern. In wealth management, privacy is treasured and insisted upon. Clients come to us assured that every interaction is treated with the utmost confidentiality. This trust is fundamental to building a healthy and long-lasting relationship in which both client and advisor are empowered to be truthful and direct.

In researching this book, the interviewees were remarkably trusting and open with stories about their experiences. We are grateful for their candor; without it this book would not be possible. In return, it was imperative to us that we respect their privacy by offering absolute anonymity.

Every anecdote that is recounted in this book actually happened. While some of the details about where or when these incidents took place have been changed, the spirit of the experience is intact. We focus on the core messages that were communicated to us in these life stories. Many specific details are included so that the stories retain their vigor and immediacy, but some of these details have been altered in order to mask the identity of the storyteller. In each instance, the intent of what was communicated to us remains the same.

These interviews were recorded so that we could accurately reflect what we were told. Each quote is verbatim.

The time is now

Clients come to us looking to solve a host of technical and logistical challenges related to managing their wealth and are not as focused on the long-lasting effect that messages around money have on their children. It's not that they don't recognize problems exist or that they may crop up in the future; it's that these issues can feel intractable and private. Also, it is often not obvious to parents that there is significant causality between wealth and a child's failure to launch. It comes as a nasty surprise that wealth itself is often responsible for creating problems in the first place. As a consequence, parents frequently push these issues aside. The intention is to get to them eventually, but these efforts invariably take a back seat to immediate needs.

As parents, we are all guilty of getting caught up in the urgent tasks, to the detriment of the important ones. Yet we must learn to aim our sights on the long term. As you will see, this often means tolerating short-term pain for long-term gain, which is exceptionally hard for any parent to do, regardless of financial status. It is our hope that this book will show you which messages most consistently launch independent, productive adults and help you determine how best to communicate those to the next generation. Our goal is to give you the confidence, in the moment, to know you are making the right choice to insist on those messages, even if implementing them is a challenge.

This book is intended to guide you along the way and make a very difficult job a little easier. It will emphasize deliberate parenting amidst wealth—being proactive rather than reactive, so that you can lay a strong foundation upon which the next generation will flourish. We will guide you in doing the important work of examining your behavior and your expectations, committing to teaching your children through example, and having a plan in place for important milestones. The ultimate goal is to enable you to give your children valuable and formative experiences that will help them become healthy, wealthy, and wise adults.

SECTION ONE

Meet Our Interviewees (in order of appearance)

....

LOGAN: Having grown up near Seattle, Washington, Logan is now the father of two young boys and lives just outside the city. For many years, he worked in strategy at various medium-sized businesses until starting his own sportswear company. Logan has one younger brother.

CRAIG: As a child, Craig lived in a prewar Manhattan apartment in the West Village. Now in his 60's, he is a retired management consultant with three grown children who live in different parts of the U.S. Craig spends a lot of time in his house in Park City, Utah, and in Europe.

EVE: Eve is the second of three children. She grew up in a home her parents built north of San Francisco. She now lives in Los Angeles, where she works as a television producer. Eve is in her late 30's and is expecting her first child.

MARK: After making their home in a tight-knit community outside Washington, D.C., Mark's family moved to the Upper East Side when he was 13 years old. He spent most summers at his grandparents' home in Maine. With his wife, Gail, Mark is raising his two boys in a brownstone near his parents. He is a venture capitalist.

MATTEO: Immediately after graduating from high school, Matteo left his native India for the United States. An enterprising man with a talent for innovation, he became a serial entrepreneur and now lives in northern California with his daughter and wife.

JANE: Though she and her brother Stephen grew up on a horse farm in the foothills of South Carolina, Jane ended up moving to New York City after college. In her 20's, she is recently engaged and works as a high school teacher in one of the city's magnet schools.

JACK: A dedicated outdoorsman, Jack edits documentaries for a living. His childhood home was tucked into the craggy hills outside Phoenix, Arizona, and he attended boarding school in New Hampshire. He now lives in New York City with his fiancée.

SAM: The eldest child and only daughter of a Moroccan father and American mother, Sam grew up in Houston, Texas. She just landed her first post-college job in publishing, and lives in a small sublet in New York City.

DANIEL: The only boy among four siblings, Daniel spent many hours a day reading and drawing as a child. He grew up in suburban Boston. He now works as a history professor in the Midwest and spends much of his free time fishing with his family.

BILL: Bill's father owned a national chain of department stores. The flagship shop was in Chicago, Illinois, where Bill and his two siblings grew up. As a teenager, he spent many weekends working in the store and now, in his late 50's, heads his family's retail empire.

SARAH: Sarah grew up in New Orleans, and now lives in Seattle, where she works as graphic designer. She is married with two stepchildren.

HENRY: As a boy, Henry spent almost every vacation with his siblings at his maternal grandparents' compound near Kennebunkport, Maine. He grew up in the New York City suburbs and is now a producer of content for cable and broadcast television. He has two college-aged children.

DAVID: David is the older brother of Eve (see above) and Susan (below). As kids, they lived just outside San Francisco. Though he held a variety of menial jobs as a teenager, including one summer spent as a dishwasher, he is now an educational consultant. He lives in the city with his black schnauzer and is recently engaged.

TAYLOR: One of our southern clients, Taylor grew up in the Buckhead district in Atlanta, with her twin brother, Scott. Her family loved to travel. Always interested in helping others, she volunteered extensively in local hospitals as a teen and later became a doctor, and also married a doctor. Taylor has two young children.

ROSS: An only child, Ross spent his early years in the seaside town of Rockport, Massachusetts, before moving to a house on the beach in Duxbury. Now in his late 60's, he started a family shortly after finishing college and has five children between the ages of 45 and 29.

PETER: Always interested in old movies as a child, Peter now writes promotional copy for studios in Los Angeles, where he has been living since he attended college. He also writes screenplays. In his mid-30's, Peter is newly married.

GABY: After growing up in a small town in northern Florida with one younger brother, Gaby moved to Philadelphia and works as a publisher for a university press.

KENT: Now an entrepreneur, Kent started his career in the military. He has one younger brother. He grew up in Mill Valley, California, and still lives in the vicinity with his wife and three children.

JOHN: John's father worked in real estate, but John always knew he wanted to work in a creative field. He grew up in and around Boston and now runs an art gallery in New York City. He is also an artist himself, specializing in mixed media and dabbling in photography. Recently married, his wife is expecting twins.

JEREMY: Part of a family with "old money," Jeremy split his time between his father's home in New York and his mother's in Vermont. He has two siblings who both live abroad. After several decades as a banker, Jeremy is now an English teacher at a boarding school near his home in Andover, Massachusetts.

STEPHEN: Stephen's older sister is Jane (see above). They grew up on a horse farm in South Carolina, and Stephen now runs a design business in Columbia. In his 30's, Stephen is married with one child.

WILLIAM: A New York native, William's life changed when he was 13 and his father sold his import business to a Fortune 500 company and relocated the family from a third-floor Village walk-up to a Park Avenue duplex. Now in his mid-50's, William runs his own successful consulting business and lives in Darien, Connecticut. His three children live and work nearby in New York City.

SUSAN: Eve and David are Susan's older siblings (see above). Their family was based outside San Francisco. Susan has always been drawn to the business world and worked her way up from being a temp in a small venture capital partnership to becoming one of their associates.

MATTHEW: Matthew grew up in a large family near the capitol in Washington, D.C. He has two older sisters and a younger brother, all of whom still live in the Washington, D.C., area. The family traveled extensively when the children were young. Long interested in the creative arts, Matthew started his career as a teenager shooting movies and now works as a freelance videographer. He is recently married and lives in Virginia.

CHAPTER ONE

....

Lift Off: What We Mean by "Grounded"
and "Successful"

In this book, when we talk about "successful" inheritors, we are not talking about a child replicating a parent's financial success. Though it's not unheard of, it's rare for an inheritor to reach the same level of financial success as the previous generation. We are talking about elements of success that lead to contented, engaged, and productive lives. The inheritors we interviewed all have launched into independently directed lives and their sense of self-worth and satisfaction with their daily endeavors is palpable.

In recent years there has been a plethora of studies delving into the science of motivation, striving, satisfaction, curiosity, and engagement. Store shelves are replete with books analyzing what success and its presumed corollary, happiness, really mean in today's culture. Every parent wants their children to be turned on, not tuned out.

Yet, young people who have rarely been denied what they want often have trouble becoming happy adults. When parents have trouble saying no, the long-term messages that they are sending their children about goals, effort, and responsibility can be highly corrosive. How do children learn to prepare for an independent adulthood if they don't understand the value of a dollar? What happens to their spirit and drive when they realize that in grown-up life they can't always replicate the environment they grew up in? Does material wealth end up defining their experience of happiness?

In our practice, we have discovered that those inheritors who have found their feet are masters of their own rich and engaged lives. They work in satisfying and challenging jobs, which may or may not pay well. If they don't love what they do, then they love the independence that working gives them. When they encounter hurdles, they keep things in perspective and persevere. They have good, open communication with family members and with others in the community. Where money is concerned, they are not beset by guilt or driven by greed.

So what are the characteristics of success that these interviewees share?

CORE MARKERS OF A SUCCESSFUL LAUNCH

When we began our research, we had various theories about why some affluent children launch successfully into life while others don't. There were patterns that we were seeing in our offices that suggested certain core messages were being lost in the mix. By talking to adult children we consider to be grounded and independent, we sought to test these theories by observing the effects of real life on real people. We wanted to identify some of the common experiences our interviewees had shared, and determine where their experiences differed and why. Most of all, we wanted to see if there were consistent themes among the experiences and core messages they felt had contributed to their success. What we discovered is in this book.

Among the many stories we heard, we identified four common threads. Children are well launched into adult life when they:

- have a demonstrated ability to earn their own money,

- are motivated toward achieving personal goals,

- have a solid sense of self that is not wrapped up in issues related to wealth, and

- can overcome setbacks.

Success is not finite. Just as a parent's job is not over when a child leaves home, so too is the work of striving toward living a satisfying life never complete. The goal for wealthy parents is to launch their children into the world so these stewards of the future can begin the work of directing their own lives, according to their own values, and striving toward their own goals.

1. The ability to earn their own money

Just a couple of decades ago, the expectation that children would take financial responsibility for their lives after college was the norm in Western countries. Then came the great recession and the term *boomerang generation* was born, describing the increasingly common practice of grown children returning to their childhood homes after college.

When there are so many good excuses to fall back on—a

tough job market or the exorbitant cost of living, for instance—
it's hard for *any* parent to insist on financial independence, let
alone parents of means. But for adult children, living off parental
income can carry emotional freight that is rarely articulated but
keenly felt. Tension about money is seldom about the money
itself or the things money can buy, but about what the money
symbolizes. For inheritors, money often represents love, security,
self-esteem, and connectedness. When they are beholden to their
parents for rent checks, spending money, or clothing allowances,
inheritors feel trapped in their parents' clutches. We heard again
and again in our interviews that adult children of the wealthy do
not *feel* successful unless they are making their own money.

And it's not enough to believe you can make money if you
need to. We found that in order to launch successfully, inheritors
needed to have *demonstrated the ability* to make money in the
past (even if they were demonstrating this to no one but themselves). There is a significant difference between assuming you
have earning power and actually experiencing getting paid for
your skills. We often hear inheritors say, "But I can get a job if I
ever really need to," and sometimes this is indeed true. But when
inheritors have never been tested, the uncertainty about whether
they could succeed can seriously undermine their confidence, and
they often find that belief and reality do not match up.

We have learned that it is remarkable what children are
capable of doing when parents simply present it to them as an
expectation. The inheritors we interviewed all took for granted
that they would earn their own money because their parents had
encouraged them to do so from an early age onwards. Yet this is
an infrequent scenario in wealthy families for two obvious
reasons. First, inconvenience: work is often difficult to fit into a
hectic schedule, and parents feel responsible for keeping
kids organized and getting them to work on time. Second, the

majority of wealthy parents (especially wealth generators) feel compelled to make their children's lives "easier." They hate to see their children suffer, struggle, or miss out on the fun elsewhere, and so they prioritize other experiences and underplay the importance of the child experiencing earning an income.

It is all too easy to fall into the trap of wanting to bail your children out—and before you know it they are on a financial drip feed. This erodes self-esteem to such an extent that the adult child's level of overall satisfaction in life is drastically reduced. We have come to believe that wealthy parents must redefine what it means to "help" their children, and understand that setting limits helps them in a more fundamental and longer-term way. Our interviewees revealed a fascinating truth: Wealthy children felt most successful when they had a career that paid a living wage, were living largely within their own means, and felt as if they would be able to support their basic needs if the family money were to disappear tomorrow. The implications of this are potentially earth shattering for a wealth industry intent on transferring wealth to the next generation, because our interviewees were actually happiest—most "successful"—when they were using very little of the wealth they inherited.

2. Motivation toward a personal goal

What does it take to be satisfied with the life you lead? The neurologist Viktor Frankl, a Holocaust survivor, determined that even in the most dire circumstances people can persevere and at times even thrive when they are fueled by a sense of purpose. This led Frankl to conclude that humankind's primary drive is not toward pleasure or happiness, but the discovery and pursuit of meaning. "What man actually needs is not a tensionless state but rather the striving and struggling for some goal worthy of him," Frankl wrote. "What he needs is not the discharge of tension at any cost, but the call of a potential meaning waiting to be fulfilled by him."[2]

Recent research supports this theory, showing that having purpose and meaning increases overall well-being and life satisfaction, improves mental and physical health, increases resiliency and self-esteem, and decreases the likelihood of suffering from depression.

The successful inheritors we interviewed all showed a remarkable ability to set explicit goals for themselves—whether it was running an art gallery, practicing medicine, or heading the family retail chain—and to commit to working toward that goal. The factor that determined an individual's sense of fulfillment and satisfaction was not necessarily achieving the goal, but successfully driving toward it. As recent research on brain function shows, working toward a goal and making progress toward its realization does more than simply activate positive feelings; it also diminishes negative emotions such as fear and depression. In many ways, it's the genuine and sustained effort that counts more than the outcome.

For many of us, the drive to make money is a major motivator and contributes directly to a sense of purpose. The wealthy naturally sometimes lack this fundamental drive. However, we all, regardless of how financially well off we are, invariably discover that making money does not always correlate with a sense of personal fulfillment because it does not automatically confer a sense of *meaning* onto our lives.

So where does meaning come from, then? It arises when we determine what interests and activities fuel us as individuals, and when we're able to pursue specific goals related to achieving those desires. This requires both skill and determination. The skill lies in having a good understanding not only of our personality, likes, and dislikes, but also of our capabilities. It takes considerable maturity and practice to understand what makes us tick *and* to have a realistic perspective on whether we can credibly hope to attain the goals we have set for ourselves.

Successful inheritors have personalities that push them toward exploration. Constantly learning encourages neural plasticity, which strengthens and creates nerve connections in our brains. Stanford researcher Carol Dweck, Ph.D., calls this having a growth mindset. "People with a growth mindset don't just seek challenge, they thrive on it,"[3] she writes. "People with a growth mindset . . . admire effort, for no matter what your ability is, effort is what ignites the ability and turns it into accomplishment."[4]

We often see inheritors who seem stuck in the status quo. They have trouble engaging fully in everyday life and finding motivation to apply themselves consistently toward achieving a goal. These individuals end up lacking a sense of success. This can be tragically debilitating. Yet in the case of our successful interviewees, each one was motivated by some desire—whether it was making money, acknowledgment in a creative field, or pursuing a deeply held interest—that drove them to apply themselves and to experience a sense of earned success that allowed them to lead productive and engaged lives.

3. A grounded sense of self

Children naturally seek to please their elders, and this often involves trying to emulate their parents or fulfill the expectations they have set. Yet affluent children often experience a sense of guilt (as well as gratitude) for the opportunities they have been afforded, and can fall into the trap of focusing their efforts in areas that speak more to their parents' goals than their own. Family wealth specialist and estate attorney Jay Hughes writes extensively about the heavy responsibility many inheritors carry in trying to integrate two sometimes conflicting missions: fulfilling their own dreams while staying true to the dreams of the wealth creator.[5] Separating one's identity as a person from the identity of one's family is a difficult enterprise for every maturing child, and it is made all the more challenging when issues of wealth are concerned.

Among the primary hurdles we all face in reaching psychological maturity is becoming comfortable in our own skin. This means we are able to accept and nurture our individual identities. We neither feel compelled to rebel against our parents or against authority, nor do we feel pressured to comply with all that these entities represent. A healthy self-identity comes when we know ourselves and our goals, and are not overly wrapped up in our parents' perceptions of us or dependent on their approval. Emotionally self-sufficient people understand their strengths and their weaknesses. They are able to take ownership of their fears, reactions, and motivations—and are able to relate to other people's feelings, fears, and reactions. Because they are confident in their ability to adapt, survive, and thrive, self-sufficient people also relate well to their environment. These are all important factors in launching successfully into an independent adult life.

With inheritors, this cycle of development is often interrupted. Adult children can feel guilty for the advantages they have enjoyed and fail to develop healthy self-esteem. They may have been saved so often from learning through their mistakes that they have trouble with perseverance, motivation, and self-discipline. Their experiences may be so different from the norm that they feel alienated and suspicious, leading them to be wary and uncertain adults.

As a result, in our field we regularly see children struggling to develop a defined and differentiated sense of self. Their identities are so wrapped up in the family wealth that they have trouble asserting their own needs and preferences. What can happen as a consequence is that adult children spend inordinate amounts of time looking backwards rather than forwards. We all know of the advantaged child who cannot look ahead to the possibilities open to them, but rather needs to assign blame for all they perceive to have gone wrong in the past. There is an acute and debilitating inability to assume responsibility for their own actions, or inactions, as these children have never conclusively separated emotionally from the older generation. The relationship between parent and child becomes dominated by the disappointment and frustration the inheritor is feeling. Their perceived lack of power quickly leads to anger and often to outright accusation.

Where some hit a roadblock that won't allow them to move forward with their lives, creating an uncomfortable environment in which they are financially *and* emotionally dependent on their parents, others are able to find a greater sense of peace where their family money is concerned. They have arrived at a healthy belief in self-reliance. Money does not govern every discussion and every decision; rather, it has assumed its appropriate place among the many concerns of daily life and does not cause undue stress.

Successful children of wealth own the privilege and the opportunity, without expecting it or taking it for granted. Internally motivated, they drive forward toward their own goals.

These qualities apply to the successful inheritors profiled in these pages, too: They are comfortable with their relationship to money and do not define themselves according to how much they do or don't have. In many ways, their family wealth is incidental. It is their sense of personal engagement and motivation that drives them most urgently in life.

4. The ability to overcome setbacks

We all want problems solved so that we can get on with our lives—but why do some people face challenges head on, with a sense of hope and tenacity, while others run away from difficulties or expect someone else to come to the rescue? The keys to sticking things through are resilience and discipline, traits that are elemental in steering individuals through the maze of adult life and enabling them to emerge at the other end with their spirits intact.

Resilience is defined as "the speedy recovery from problems," and its most apt synonym is *flexibility*. It is a trait that is essential for all children and adults, regardless of financial status. While money can alleviate many problems, it cannot help us develop good relationships with others, make us more effective at work, or give us the strength to see beyond a personal tragedy and forge ahead regardless.

A complicating factor is that coping with and overcoming adversity is a core skill that is developed experientially, over a period of time. In the case of inheritors, if they lack this ability by the time they reach adulthood, engineering the experiences that may help them develop it can be arduous and unsuccessful. It is therefore all the more critical that from an early age onwards, wealthy parents provide their children with consistent opportunities to deal with the consequences of their actions and the actions of others.

Yet children of means are often stymied because they are spared having to muddle through managing their own problems. Time and again, they are saved from the consequences of their errors by well-meaning parents, and so they never have a chance to learn from their own mistakes. As a result, they cannot adequately build up their internal resources to address problems that might arise in the future, engaging instead in a vicious cycle of incompetence that makes them even more dependent on others.

Sadly, this is all too frequent a scenario in the wealth management industry. Too many affluent children struggle to take effective action to solve problems, and instead choose the easy way out. Most often, this is reflected in their career trajectories, where they quit as soon as a job becomes boring or difficult. If they don't need to work for money, then why stick it out?

Recent studies from the University of Pennsylvania[6] reveal that high scores in self-discipline are better predictors of future success than IQ scores. This finding has enormous implications because discipline can be taught. It is possible to encourage kids to be focused and develop a perspective that allows them to strive for longer-term, more abstract goals. Here's what the study revealed: In an exceedingly boring coding test which required no particular intelligence but a willingness to persevere—to stand up to the challenge of boredom—those participants with low IQs who did well on the test were proven to find greater professional success later in life than the smart kids who didn't score as well because they didn't try as hard. The labor market values the kind of internal motivation and diligence that is needed to do well on a test like this, even when there's no external reward. It measures the important noncognitive skills that have a huge impact on success in the real world.

The inheritors we spoke with all exhibited an attitude of optimism and self-sufficiency that drove them to commit to goals and strive toward fulfilling them regardless of the immediate rewards. They showed resilience and discipline in spades, believing that, by their own efforts, any problem could be adequately addressed and overcome. As we will see, when parents allow their children to take charge by teaching them that the results they produce depend on their own efforts and actions, they are imparting a lifelong gift. These children will be able to weather challenges and constantly grow their capabilities.

Through many stories, these adult children of wealth demonstrated an inner strength founded upon the core elements of a successful launch that we have outlined: demonstrated earning ability, personal motivation, resiliency, and a grounded sense of self.

When an individual reveals through their actions flexibility of attitude, creativity in problem solving, enthusiasm, and a good work ethic, they are much better prepared to handle the inevitable challenges that adult life will throw in their direction. "The good life is best construed as a matrix that includes happiness, occasional sadness, a sense of purpose, playfulness, and psychological flexibility, as well autonomy, mastery, and belonging," wrote researchers Robert Biswas-Diener and Todd B. Kashdan in *Psychology Today*. "Parsing the good life into a matrix is more than linguistic trickery; shifting toward a mixed-bag view of well-being opens more paths to achieving a personally desirable life."[7]

But in order for parents to help their children develop this definition of a good life, they must first develop a high tolerance for watching their children struggle and perhaps even fail. Only in allowing their children to recover from these setbacks through their own concerted efforts can parents help them realize that they do in fact possess untapped resilience and capability.

Growing up healthy, wealthy, and wise

Parents today are engaged in a full-time battle with modern consumerism, and the wealthy parent's struggles are all the harder for never having to say no. These days, even parents with little money shower their children with possessions and services, whether it's endless plastic trinkets available from fast-food restaurants, ubiquitous designer jeans, or manicures for tots. Unlike previous generations, ours believes that we deserve luxuries and have earned them, even if we cannot truly afford them. This makes it all the harder for affluent parents to raise children who launch into adulthood grounded and sensible, with the ability to forge ahead with psychological and economic independence.

A disproportionate focus on material goods, ease, and comfort distracts children from becoming successful achievers. Achievers are more likely to find balance and happiness in intangibles such as earned self-esteem, ownership of their efforts and successes, and emotional control. "Giving your child a fundamental belief in him- or herself. Allowing your child to gain ownership of his or her achievements in life. Teaching your child to be an emotional master. Raising your child to be a successful achiever," writes Dr. James Taylor, an expert in the psychology of performance in his book *Positive Pushing*. "These are the greatest gifts that you can give your child. Yet they are also the most difficult gifts to achieve."[8]

Our call to action to parents of means is to choose to commit to imparting messages to your children that will help them lead productive and happy lives, rather than allowing serendipity to dictate outcomes. In focusing on adult children who have absorbed powerful lessons from their parents and found ways to implement those lessons into their daily lives, thereby creating meaningful existences for themselves, it is our hope that you, too, can consider these messages and put them to good use in your family.

Intentional parenting is hard work, and includes infinite challenges and rewards. Let's turn our attention now to the many inheritors who exemplify success in its various manifestations, and see what messages are most profound and ring most true.

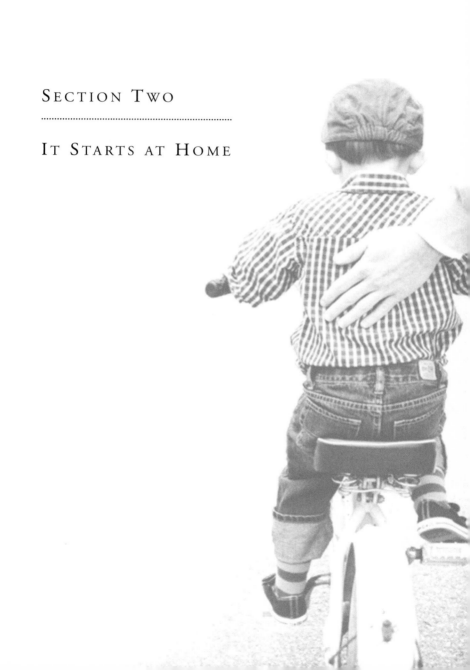

Section Two

It Starts at Home

CHAPTER TWO

....

Allow Your Child to Strive—Don't Buy Their Success

Is there a parent on earth—wealthy or not—who doesn't want their child to be independent and happy? As Stanford psychologist Carol Dweck says, most parents think, "'I would do anything, give anything, to make my children successful,'" and yet, "many of the things they do boomerang."[9] We see this problem played out most starkly in affluent families: While the family funds are often tapped with the express purpose of supporting the next generation's success, these efforts can backfire when the money and the opportunities it buys instead rob the young adults of the desire and ability to find their own success.

Yet, through their stories and actions, many of our wealthy inheritors revealed the kind of innate drive that lead them to strive for and achieve success on their own terms. How did they find the will to do so? We identified several significant commonalities among their stories. Their parents taught them about limits, whether through seemingly inconsequential daily decisions or through momentous turning points. The inheritors learned through experiencing the consequences of their own behavior and as a result were given the opportunity to discover their own inventiveness and resilience. Parents took the long view, steeling themselves against short-term inconveniences and worries. As we will see, even though in each of these cases the immediate consequences were oftentimes painful and uncertain, the children absorbed the underlying message about the value of effort. They grew up determined, resilient, and grateful.

There's an often-told myth that tells of how eagles build their nests when preparing for the arrival of their young, which like many myths, holds a powerful message. First, the father collects rocks and branches, often with thorns attached, and creates an underlayer. On top of this, he builds up a softer pad made of grasses and feathers. When the baby eagles are born, they have a chance to mature in comfort, protected from predators. While living in the nest, they are helpless, weak, and passive. Then there comes a time when they begin to outgrow the confines of the nest but don't yet know how to fly, let alone hunt down their own food.

It's at this point that the mother eagle begins to strip down the soft padding that cushions the nest. As the eaglets teeter on the edge, afraid to launch into the air for the first time, she is busy exposing the thorns and rocks and sharp branches. When the baby eagles fall back, they no longer find the familiar and the comfortable embracing them. In this way they are urged to literally take flight.

In much the same way, human parents must prepare their children for life in the real world as independent adults. We hope these stories will give you ideas on how and when to begin stripping the nest of its padding.

Can a childhood be too easy?

There seems to be a mysterious epidemic of unhappy young adults in the Western world. These are children raised in relative affluence who have had joyous childhoods, attentive parents, and never suffered trauma or heartbreak; in other words, they have nothing to complain about. Everything suggests they should be teed up for happy adulthood, and yet they're not. Therapist and author Lori Gottlieb writes in *The Atlantic* about seeing a flood of these unsettled, privileged youth in her practice. It was all the more perplexing because their parents, she explains, "had always been 'attuned' . . . and had made sure to guide my patients through any and all trials and tribulations of childhood."[10]

Yet she was seeing grown children who suffered depression and anxiety, had difficulty choosing or committing to a satisfying career path, struggled with relationships, and felt a sense of emptiness and a lack of purpose. While they had the freedom to find themselves and the encouragement to do anything they wanted in life, they felt listless and unfulfilled as adults. Their parents drove carpools, helped with homework, intervened when children were bullied, paid for music lessons and enrichment opportunities, and talked through difficult feelings. So why the persistent unease in these children once they reached adulthood? Gottlieb began to ask herself: "Could it be that by protecting our kids from unhappiness as children, we're depriving them of happiness as adults?"[11]

Put another way: Do parents really do too much for their kids nowadays? We all want to help our children, but the real question is *help them do what?* Help them avoid difficulties and consequences, or help them surmount difficulties and anticipate consequences? Gottleib argues that by trying so hard to provide the perfectly happy childhood, parents are making it harder for their kids to actually grow up.

This problem is compounded for children raised in wealth. As child psychologist and educator Madeline Levine, author of *The Price of Privilege*, writes, "America's newly identified at-risk group is preteens and teens from affluent, well-educated families."[12] Yet, as we will see, being a member of this surprising risk group does not necessarily doom you to failure.

Take Logan, for example, who grew up near Seattle, Washington, and was the oldest of two boys. Like any suburban teenager, he was excited to pass his driver's test and enjoy the freedom of driving himself around instead of having to rely on others. Even though his parents could easily have afforded to buy him a car, a few years before his 16th birthday his father made him a proposal: "For every two dollars you save toward a car, I'll give you one."

By the time Logan passed his test and turned 16, he'd saved up $1,500, and with the extra $750 from his father, he was able to buy himself a dark blue used Toyota. In contrast, his father did not make this same offer to Logan's younger brother. Instead, he bought the Toyota from Logan and gave it to his other son.

For a variety of reasons, "[my brother] wasn't treated the same and he didn't learn the same lessons," Logan explained. "To this day he resents me for having things and doing things he doesn't have or do. He hasn't grasped the concept of working hard for what you want." The father's act of planning ahead taught his older son how to strive for something, whereas he enabled the younger son in a way that ended up robbing him of his sense of ability and agency. Even within the same family, it's all too easy to send the wrong messages and miss the chance to teach children the value of striving toward a goal. And when that family is one of means, it's even easier to fall into the trap of buying their happiness and "success" rather than letting them earn it.

Avoiding the negative influences of affluence

When parents are so deeply invested in their children's lives, they can fall into the trap of trying to smooth out every rough patch. Ironically, this inability to let go often signals a lack of trust: *We don't think you can handle this on your own.* As we saw with Logan's brother, when parents do not believe a child can handle certain responsibilities it almost guarantees that the child will indeed live down to those expectations; it ends up undermining them.

Living in affluence makes navigating this launch into adulthood even harder. For instance, it is far more challenging for parents to set limits when a child can simply claim, "but everyone else has one" or "everyone goes there." And when "we can't afford it" isn't a reasonable assertion, it's much harder to say no to purchases and opportunities. Having money also means it's almost impossible to resist helping your child out of a bind, say if they lose their expensive athletic equipment and you buy them a replacement so they won't miss the game and disappoint the coach or the players. In this case, not helping feels like you are *depriving* the child. However, a family of lesser means would not even have the option of replacing the equipment and so would not suffer from any guilt.

The message that affluent children hear all too often is that money can solve their problems. They see that extreme wealth buys a lot of "yeses." Wealthy young adults get special treatment from educational institutions that admit them even if they are less than qualified. Employers interview candidates they otherwise never would have bothered with, just because of a family's influence. Pretty soon, the child is encapsulated in a fantasy world and left wholly ill prepared to function in the real world if and when they are asked to strike out on their own.

One reason the eagle myth persists is that it succinctly reminds us that limit-setting and enforced hardship are necessary for the next generation to launch (literally).

The question then becomes, *how do we do this in reality?* It boils down to a deceptively simple list of to-dos:

- Love your child enough to set limits.

- Don't rescue your child. Allow them to fail and/or experience the logical consequences of their behavior and recover. Encourage them to make their own decisions and to live with the consequences.

- Yes, be supportive, but do so in a way that rewards them when they strive to succeed, rather than eliminates the need for them to strive in the first place.

But how does this play out day-to-day? When your child doesn't get into the private school that you wanted them to attend, do you make a phone call or not? When they blow through the credit card limit and have no money of their own to pay off the balance, and no job to earn back the money, what steps do you take? This chapter will show you how to respond to these situations and others, revealing how our interviewees were encouraged to *strive to succeed.*

Parents Need to Balance "Yes" with "No"

Parents instinctively want to avoid conflict to make life easier and happier in the immediate term, yet conflict is often where real learning begins. For wealthy parents it's all too easy to say "yes" to everything without thinking through long-term consequences. When parents are too lenient, the lack of discipline and consequences hurts their children. From letting kids throw their clothes on the floor to replenishing the account when the child has gone over budget, there is an almost daily barrage of circumstances where a yes is easier but a no is what is needed in the long run.

While on an intellectual level parents know that giving their children everything they ask for can't possibly be good for them, on an emotional level it's a different story. What parents don't realize is that by saying no and providing limits, they are in fact showing their children that they care enough about them and their long-term development to disagree with them in the moment.

The revelation for many parents is that saying "no" can be an extremely helpful experience. Children who have few financial limitations often lead lives with less parental oversight. Parents outsource many of the logistics by using nannies, drivers, and tutors, and so there are fewer opportunities to place limits on the children's behavior and activities. But when a parent takes the time to be involved, making the effort to disagree, take an unpopular stand, or simply say no, they are actively showing their child their love.

Why "no" is necessary

As a child, Craig grew up in Manhattan and spent winter vacations skiing in the mountains out West. After marrying and having two boys and a girl, Craig decided to build his own house outside Park City, Utah, so he and his young family could spend their free time together outdoors. Their house was conveniently located near the ski slopes but not far from the city where they enjoyed an active cultural life during the off seasons.

Eventually, Craig's middle child, Kylie, graduated from college and decided to try to become a writer. The house in Park City was empty most of the year as the oldest and youngest sons had demanding jobs on the East Coast, and Craig and his wife, Ann, were spending more and more time in Europe. They allowed Kylie to move in temporarily, thinking she would be there for a few months while she looked for a job and worked on her first novel. Those months stretched into a year. They knew they had a serious problem on their hands when Kylie was still living in the house, rent free, 18 months after graduating.

"My daughter picked up messages about having a lot of wealth that have registered in her mind," said Craig, who admitted to regretting that he did not establish clearer limits early enough. One morning when he and Ann were visiting, they gathered around the kitchen island drinking coffee and laid down the law.

"We told her she had to move out. It was the first and only moment of fear in her life . . . her eyes grew wide when we stood there and told her." They helped her find and pay for an apartment in New York City, and gave her one year to figure out how to take over the rent. "It was not easy for her, but she did do it."

For wealthy parents, it is necessary to balance all the "yeses" their children hear with the occasional parental "no." Take Eve, who grew up in Northern California. Twice a year her mother would take her to San Francisco to go clothes shopping, followed by lunch at a downtown bistro. "We had a budget," Eve said. "My mom would pick out the clothes. She'd say, 'You can get this but not this.'" Her parents wanted their children to have great experiences, but they also wanted to balance out those experiences with reality checks so the kids would develop a grounded perspective.

But saying no is rarely easy. Ultimately, it's about finding the right balance. "On one hand, the undisciplined child will constantly create stress, frustration and anger . . . and may grow into adulthood at risk for serious behavioral problems," writes wealth psychologist Lee Hausner in *Children of Paradise.* "On the other hand, the overly disciplined child may interpret constant parental punishment as rejection and loss of love . . . [and] the child will ultimately develop a very low self-esteem and be equally at risk for serious behavioral problems."[13]

Saying no to children and seeing through consequences is a challenge that all parents must face, regardless of their wealth status—but it may be even more important for children of means. Unless they learn to live within limits, this elite population risks growing into adults who are constantly at odds with the world. "Rules, they believe," writes Dr. Hausner, "are simply for others."[14] When this happens, wealthy adult children find excuses and justifications for everything, and may fail to learn how to succeed on their own in the real world.

Help children by simplifying choices

Oftentimes, children need parents to help them narrow down their options. As Swarthmore Professor Barry Schwartz, author of *The Paradox of Choice* explains, too many options can be so confusing as to be debilitating. "Autonomy and freedom . . . are critical to our well-being, and choice is critical to freedom and autonomy," he writes. "Nonetheless, though modern Americans have more choice than any group of people ever has before, and thus, presumably, more freedom and autonomy, we don't seem to be benefiting from it psychologically."[15] As such, while explicit parental direction is often what the child thinks he or she doesn't want, it is in fact just what they need.

We saw this simplification of options play out in Mark's childhood experiences. Until he turned 13, his family had lived in a tight-knit community on the outskirts of Washington, D.C. When his father took over as the head of a large conglomerate, they moved to Manhattan's Upper East Side and bought a townhouse, which they restored. Living in the city among a cadre of wealthy children was new for Mark. His parents gave him an allowance of $20 a week when all around him, kids were getting hundreds to spend.

The city was an extraordinary playground: There were endless movies to see, shops to explore, cafés to hang out in. Everywhere he turned, Mark encountered yet another opportunity to do something new or buy something cool. "I saw kids spending money without knowing where it came from or what they were getting," he said. But living in a big city with virtually no limits on what they could experience or purchase, these children frequently found themselves bored and listless. When everything is possible, sometimes nothing seems appealing. Mark, in contrast, learned to live within his means and always felt he had something concrete to strive for. "I had to spend wisely; I couldn't always have everything I wanted," he said.

As we will see, another way of narrowing down the overwhelming options is by allowing children to live with their mistakes.

DON'T RESCUE YOUR CHILD

In the parenting bestseller *The Blessing of a Skinned Knee*, L.A. clinical psychologist Wendy Mogel argues that parents' good intentions are doing their children serious harm. "When we treat our children's lives like we're cruise ship directors who must get them to their destination—adulthood—smoothly without their feeling even the slightest bump or wave," she writes, "we're depriving them."[16] She explains that in her practice she sees endless children who have been pushed to succeed at all costs and were never allowed to fail. They never learned to strive.

Yet if parents would allow children to learn by doing and sometimes failing, these children would better accept the consequences of their actions, and grow up to be more realistic and flexible—characteristics that contribute to enjoying a balanced and happy life. "By giving them a chance to survive some danger and letting them make some reckless or thoughtless choices, we teach them how to withstand the bumps and knocks of life. This is the only way children will mature into resilient, self-reliant adults,"[17] Dr. Mogel explains.

What lies at the core of this parental dilemma about whether or not to allow children to fail? According to the authors of *Facilitating Financial Health,* it's guilt. Parents ask themselves how they can allow their children or grandchildren to suffer when the family has more than enough money to help them. Driven by self-reproach and the desire to protect, wealthy parents easily fall into the trap of playing the eternal "fixer." When this is carried on into adulthood and the wealthy parents continually bail out their adult children, this can "create resentment and anger on the part of the parents or other siblings, a sense of entitlement or resentment on the part of the recipients; a lack of motivation, passion, innovation, creativity, and drive for financial dependents; and mutual frustrations that can damage relationships."[18]

And unless they overcome hurdles by their own efforts, these children will never know that they really do have it in them to bounce back. To grow up and be able to face normal adult hurdles, children need to experience failure and learn how to recover from it.

Let them take responsibility for their own mistakes

Matteo is a cheerful man with a wide smile. After deciding he needed to make a life for himself in a country where his family was not well known, he struck out on his own. His story of moving from India to the United States at age 18 is astonishing for many reasons, but mostly because he exhibited atypical confidence and resilience at such an early age, especially for a child raised in such rarefied circles. Once he left home, he never again relied on financial support from his family, yet over the years managed to build up his own art collecting business worth many millions.

In reflecting on how he developed his unusual poise and positivity, Matteo recalled a seminal experience when he was a teenager. Early one Saturday morning in February, he headed to an elite private school in a nearby town to sit for an entrance exam. Though he hadn't given it much thought or effort, later when he received the letter saying he had failed the exam and would not be admitted to the school, he was astonished and offended. "I went to my father and told him to call them and get me in," he said. "My parents laughed at me."

They told him his only hope of getting in would be to study harder for the exam and take it again in April. "I was definitely left with the impression that it was sink or swim." Matteo applied himself to the work the second time around, and gained acceptance under his own steam. That experience fueled his confidence, whereas if his parents had swooped in and saved him it would likely have had just the opposite effect.

Jane is a young inheritor in her 20's who, like Matteo, understood as a young adult that true independence would be the key to her happiness. Her family owned a horse farm nestled in the rolling hills of South Carolina. One spring, over a series of fun weekends when she was 16 years old, Jane racked up a bill of $1,000 on her credit card—spending that had not been authorized by her parents. Instead of allowing her to get away with it, they insisted she pay every penny back that summer by doing chores around the house and helping on the farm by cleaning horse stalls for $7 an hour. Her parents required her to log in 40 hours a week "because I needed to get used to having a normal job, and those were the hours of a normal job," Jane explained. Once she made enough money to repay them, she found someone else to do the work for them.

"How long it took me to pay them back taught me the value of a dollar," she said. "Dad didn't make me feel bad about it; there was just no other option. He said, 'These weren't approved charges. You need to pay me back.'" There was no judgment about what she had spent the money on, just a simple line drawn in the sand.

"Parents help their children develop self-management skills by setting limits, modeling self-control, and being clear about the value of tolerating frustration, delaying gratification and controlling impulses," writes Levine, author of *The Price of Privilege*. "The ability to self-manage effectively is a great predictor of both psychological adjustment and academic achievement,"[19] Dr. Levine says.

Let them learn about causality

Remember Eve, whose mother took her clothes shopping twice a year? In fifth grade, Eve's friend told her about a great sleep-away camp that she'd attended where they got to rappel down cliffs and sleep in the wild. She thought it sounded amazing and persuaded her parents to allow her to sign up for four weeks in the summer between elementary and middle school. A somewhat quiet child, Eve would really come alive when engaged in an activity she loved. But a few days before she was supposed to head off to camp, Eve got cold feet and begged her parents to allow her to stay home.

They were taken aback. The full fee for the camp tuition had already been paid, but money wasn't the only problem—it was that their daughter had made a commitment to go. Eve remembers her father being so upset with her for wanting to renege on going that he backed his car into the garage. After a family discussion, her parents decided she had to follow through.

"It was probably a good thing that they sent me," she said. Helping her recognize that she did indeed have the courage to see through her obligation gave Eve the confidence to leave home for a semester abroad a few years later. "If I'd chickened out of going to camp, I think I might not have gone to Europe in high school." Not only did she learn about causality, but she also learned that she was more adaptive and adventurous than shy and fearful.

Often, these lessons are less about surviving a grand moment of failure or drama and more about navigating mundane, day-to-day activities. Take driving a car, for instance. If your child drives regularly, he or she will need money to fill the gas tank. The child will either need to allocate money from his or her allowance, or get a job to earn the money needed for refueling. If the parents simply hand over a prepaid credit card for gas, they rob the child of a wealth of lessons about real life contained in this simple daily occurrence. Many of our interviewees remembered this equation—*If I want to drive a car, I'll need to pay for gas*—as instrumental in helping them understand the causal link between their actions and their consequences. Incidentally, it also taught them about the value of money, and how much better it was when they had their own money rather than continually having to ask for it.

What, then, should parents ask themselves in the moment to help them make these decisions about where to draw the line? A simple test is to try to make home life mimic the real world as much as possible: If the real world would charge rent, parents should, too. If children are trying to raise money for a business, let them go out and raise that money from someone other than you, and make sure your contribution is among the *smallest*, not the *largest*. Avoid creating a world in which you are buying your child special treatment in an effort to facilitate their successes—it's far more effective to teach them to strive, as this allows them to earn success for themselves.

The key here is being able to see the challenges that this mimicking of the real world brings as formative rather than debilitating. If parents see these experiences as debilitating, it suggests they don't believe their child can handle it. Kids pick up on this lack of confidence in their capabilities.

You can do it!

Children love being able to do things on their own, and when they make a mistake and discover that they can recover from it, they develop self-confidence. Harvard psychologist and author of *Too Much of a Good Thing*, Dan Kindlon, says this powerful confidence helps them develop "psychological immunity," which prepares them for the inevitable vicissitudes of adulthood.

"What we want for our children is a perfect life devoid of hardship and pain," Kindlon says. "But their happiness as adults is largely dependent on the tools we give them, tools that will allow them to develop emotional maturity—to be honest with themselves, to be empathetic, to take initiative, to delay gratification, to learn from failure and move on, to accept their flaws, and to face the consequences when they've done something wrong."[20]

Now an adult with two young children of his own, Logan—whose father matched his savings so he could buy his first car—recalls seeing many of the parents in the Seattle neighborhood where he grew up throwing money around to bail their kids out whenever they got in trouble. Instead of letting the school punish them for cheating, the parents made phone calls to call off the heat. If the kids had a car accident, the parents hired lawyers to expunge their record. "Kids would do catastrophically stupid things and their families would swoop in and save them," Logan said. In his family, he knew this was not an option. "If I screwed up it was going to be on me."

What he learned from having to tough out the consequences of his own behavior was that he needed strength of character and resilience to forge ahead. "Failure is probably a better teacher than success. It builds character."

Take Off the Kid Gloves—But Steel Yourself

When parents feel that they don't want to see their children suffer, what do they actually mean by "suffer"? When a child is forced to live within a budget, is that suffering? When she can't get the latest model car, does that constitute deprivation? When he lives in a cramped apartment, is that too much to expect him to bear? All suffering is relative.

Over the years of working with affluent families, we have learned again and again that it is imperative not to protect wealthy children from "real" life. "Suffering" builds resilience, and encourages children to strive to change their circumstances. When wealthy parents protect their kids while enabling them to live a lifestyle they can't afford, they are undermining the development of the children's desire to succeed. By enabling the successful outcome they have rid the child of the need to strive.

Young people need to learn through real-life experiences, even if—and sometimes *especially* if—these experiences are hard. Wealth advisor Ellen Miley Perry explains in her book *A Wealth of Possibilities* that parents have "worked so hard to attain freedom and security that they, quite naturally, wish to create more ease in the lives of their children. These parents are often seeking ways to help their children figure out a world that they themselves had to learn about the hard way." But instead of driving toward success and independence for their children, parents must provide them with training wheels so they can take off on their own.

"Don't create a gated community around them lest they become narrow and scared," she emphasizes. But most important of all, allow them to experience the joy and hard-earned pride of learning to manage travails on their own. "When you're left with little other than your own ingenuity and determination, you find out just how much you can really accomplish. What a shame to take that away from a child by solving their every problem and inconvenience."[21]

Surviving a child's unhappiness

For every galvanizing story from our interviewees about their seminal learning experiences, there were worried, heartsick parents standing on the sidelines, wringing their hands over whether or not their child would weather the storm. The successes we heard were not just about the children finding their feet in tricky circumstances, but also about the parents who steeled themselves so they could survive the experience. Each time, parents had to bite their tongues, close their purses, stay neutral, or resist interfering—all the time hoping and trusting that their children would not only be all right, but would emerge all the stronger for it.

Jack grew up in the desert outside Phoenix, Arizona, surrounded by saguaros and sand. As a small child, he'd spend hours trekking in the craggy hills with his father and younger sister. Fascinated by the natural world, he spent one summer when he was a teenager working for a well-known scientist on a remote island off the coast of western Canada. Unaccustomed to the lush and remote landscape, he was excited to be studying the impact of clear cutting in that region. For two months, he assisted in cataloguing discoveries, gathering data, and helping run the base camp. There was a lot of physical labor involved and a huge amount of solitary time. It was tough for a 16-year-old. Sometimes he would be in the wilderness for five days at a stretch without seeing or talking to anyone but the scientist. "While I definitely felt a satisfaction in doing that work," he said, "it was very lonely and isolating for me to be out there for that amount of time. But I wanted to do something that was of value."

While the experience was transformative, and much of

Jack's work as an adult is closely linked to his interest in conservation, it was a difficult time for him. But in some ways, it was just as difficult for his mother. Jack remembers a picture of himself sitting alone in front of the campfire with a pained expression on his face. "To this day, my mom still can't look at the picture of me looking into the fire; it's too hard for her." She questioned whether sending him away at such a young age for so long had been the right thing to do, and worried about how unhappy he seemed. Had she expected too much of him? Would he be scarred for life?

Yet allowing Jack to try something so challenging, and to discover that he could weather the ups and downs, gave him a sense of purpose and accomplishment that he would not have felt had he spent an ordinary summer with his parents (where he would have been far more social and probably happier).

Parents need to fight against the instinct to protect their kids from harm and pain. In looking back, the children themselves often testify to what an immense learning experience it was to endure those hardships.

Swallowing your own impatience

Another of our interviewees, Samantha, discovered her own capacity for resourcefulness and persistence when it came time to find her first job out of college. Sam was the eldest child and only daughter of a father who emigrated from Morocco and a mother who came from the plains of Texas. As an undergraduate, Sam had studied English history and creative writing, and decided she wanted to find a job on the business side of the publishing industry. She spent many months looking for work. Hour after hour, day after day, she did her homework and eventually landed an entry-level position at one of the companies she had targeted early on in her search. Of all her friends, she is one of only a handful to have found paid employment within six months of graduation. "I got this job on my own," she said, her voice swelling with pride. "It's a great job. I'm living alone. I'm not totally financially independent yet, but pretty close for just being out of college!"

Her father remembers the process of Sam's job search too, but with a different emphasis. Sam came to him and asked whether he knew anyone in the publishing industry who might be able to help her get a job. While he would have been happy to oblige, as a successful financial services professional he simply didn't know anyone in her chosen field. He has a palpable memory of having to sit on the sidelines over several months, worrying about whether or not his daughter would land on her feet. He fought against his impatience and his anxiety, trying to trust that she would eventually figure it out on her own. "Being a parent, you have to incur the pain," he said, "and the pain is watching your kids struggle."

In Sam's memory, she is elated that she got the job on her own and she takes from the experience only the pride that she accomplished this very difficult feat. She doesn't lament the many months she spent looking for work or the fact that her father couldn't help her. Interestingly, her father's lack of help may have been the very impetus she needed to go out and get a job on her own. Sometimes, being tough is what kids need in order to grow up and take responsibility for themselves. Although they probably won't thank you in the moment, as adults they will benefit from having a fundamental skill set that developed as a result of their own striving.

Parents and children have different tasks. Another reason the eagle story resonates is that its portrayal of the parents is inspiring. As the fledgling eagle learns to fly, the parents have to watch it experience the pain of falling back among the thorns and endure the reality that their offspring may have trouble learning how to fly. Yet somehow, knowing what they have to do, they have the fortitude and conviction to press on.

REWARD STRIVING, WITHOUT ELIMINATING THE NEED FOR IT

Very few people, whether young or old, financially well off or struggling, enjoy discomfort. While adults have the maturity to see that beyond immediate discomfort often lies a reward—whether it's something tangible like a trimmer physique, or intangible like a feeling of competence and satisfaction—a child's natural instinct is to stop once things get hard. James Taylor, the researcher on the psychology of performance, argues that people are creatures of inertia unless a force is exerted on them. "When they first try something new," he writes, "they will often put forth effort until it gets difficult or uncomfortable."[22]

If, at that point, parents allow the child to stop trying to improve and succeed, they are denying them the chance to discover that their limits are greater than they thought. "If you push him to try harder and persist longer, 'Good job so far, but we bet you can do even better,'" Dr. Taylor writes, "he is more likely to face his discomfort and attain a higher level of achievement and satisfaction."[23] As Myra Salzer, founder of the Wealth Conservancy, writes in *The Inheritor's Sherpa*, "People don't sign up for sink or swim circumstances."[24]

If this is the case, then how should parents push their children to strive for difficult achievements without taking over the effort themselves and rewarding success rather than effort? In their desire to help, how do parents avoid eliminating the need for children to strive in the first place?

How to encourage striving

When parents have high expectations of their children, it encourages the children to internalize these high expectations and try to live up to them. "Our society is highly achievement oriented," writes Dr. Taylor in *Positive Pushing*. "If children don't learn to respond to the challenges of achievement in a positive way, they're going to have difficulty when they enter society as adults."[25]

Earlier, we met Mark who moved to New York City and learned to survive on far less allowance than his wealthy friends. Watching the effort and integrity his father brought to the table when it came to work, Mark grew up absorbing the lesson that striving to succeed could lead to great things. Each night his father shared stories about his workday, talked about the successes and failures, and encouraged Mark and his siblings to follow in his footsteps. "It's all about high standards and knowing what to expect from yourself—what to hold yourself accountable to, in school but also professionally," he said. He learned this by watching his father push himself to be the best leader he could be. "We were internalizing these standards and holding them up for our-selves. Whatever you do, you do it well. You set the goal, the end-point, that is right for yourself. You think about how far you want to take yourself—that was the message."

The expectations he now sets for himself as an adult are informed by the expectations his parents set for themselves. He is guided by the idea that the striving toward an appropriate yet challenging goal is what gives life meaning and purpose. "If you're going to go into medicine, strive to be a doctor," he said. "Aim high."

We heard a number of stories from our interviewees about parents encouraging their children to perform well in school, and holding them to these high standards. In many ways, school was seen as the child's first "job," and parents used both the carrot and the stick to ensure the child got the most from the experi-ence—the carrot in the form of privileges the child enjoyed when striving for excellence, and the stick being when the parent threat-ened to refuse privileges, such as paying for college, if the child did not apply him or herself enough.

Daniel was a bright child, the only boy among three daugh-ters. Growing up on the outskirts of Boston, he was a self-pro-fessed book nerd who also loved all things athletic. Although he was a good student, he had to work hard for his grades and his parents were clear in their high expectations. "If you play the game, get the grades, don't get in trouble, you'll get certain priv-ileges," they explained to him. They fully expected him to be on the honor roll and told him that if he managed to stay among the top students in his class through high school, they would buy him a car when he turned 17. Conversely, if things went awry they'd yank his privileges. "You'll benefit," they said, "but you will need to work for it, and if we see in any way that you're not responsible, it will be taken away in a second."

Mark, the venture capitalist, recalls how his parents communicated that they expected him to apply himself in school. His score in the 99th percentile on every standardized test he took growing up made it clear he was gifted intellectually, so his parents used to say to him, "If you're not doing well at school, it's not because you don't have the brains. It's because you're not trying hard." He internalized this message and as an adult describes it as a fundamental responsibility to apply yourself to the best of your ability to whatever you're engaged in: "Whatever you are doing, do it right."

Let the kids take the reins

When Bill was young, he loved to spend time at the photography shop a couple of blocks from his father's flagship department store in downtown Chicago. Shooting pictures and developing film became a passion of his. His parents let him set up a darkroom in his home where he spent endless hours experimenting with various development techniques. "The attic in our home was a place I could tune out of the world," he said. When he was about 13, his father decided to honor the longstanding employees in his store and hired Bill to do a photo project for him.

"I went around and took portraits of all the employees who had been there for five years or more," Bill said. "It was a labor of love and I got paid for it." When the pictures were developed, they were framed and hung in a high-traffic area at the entrance to the store, where all incoming and outgoing customers could see them.

Bill's father played no role in deciding which photos were chosen. Some of them didn't come out well and Bill decided they had to be redone. At his own expense, he took them to a special lab where they were printed on specific high-quality photo paper. "I had total ownership of that project," he said. "That taught me a valuable lesson about empowerment and allowing people to make decisions and succeed or fail."

Letting children earn success on their own requires intentional parenting as well as time and patience. When toddlers are learning to dress themselves in the morning, it takes immense patience not to step in and pull the clothes on for them, yet parents know that their child must eventually learn to do it themselves. In a similar way, parents of older children need to be patient as they create space for their children to own their successes. It takes time and forethought to make this happen. It's as though parents are creating a scaffold for their children to climb, but must then sit back and let their child do the climbing by themselves. The outcome is most successful when the child tries to scale the heights and learns through trial and error which approach is best for them.

YOUR KIDS WILL THANK YOU . . . LATER

It's always more gratifying to say yes to a child and see them smile than say no and disappoint them. Pushing children to try hard and watching them struggle or fail can be emotionally wrenching. Sometimes it's tempting to sit back and let things play themselves out, especially if youngsters are surly or unappreciative in the moment, and sometimes interfering is irresistible. In that moment when a child resists your efforts, it's hard to see that their disappointment or anger will not last, and that these negative emotions are, in fact, both developmentally appropriate and necessary to build their resilience. It is part of the process. We heard consistently from our interviewees that looking through the lens of maturity casts a much more favorable light on their experiences: Even if your kids don't love your actions in the moment, they'll thank you later.

At home, Sam's parents insisted that she and her brothers always treat them with respect. They had high expectations of how their children should behave, and held them to those standards. Frustrated, Sam would sometimes behave like a sullen teenager and roll her eyes at her parents. "Hearing it got annoying, yes, but at the end of the day, it really affected the way I act. It stunk, but it helps that they were strict. They stuck to their word." As is the case with many children, Sam is now appreciative of her parents and glad that they were tough on her; she understands that she needed that kind of guidance. "It probably helped me a lot," she said, "to know these are the rules, these are what's normal."

As a boy, Logan from Seattle sometimes felt that his father's academic expectations of him were too high. "He was always pushing me to do a little more, work a little harder." When Logan brought home his report card, he and his dad would go over it in his dad's office. "If they weren't straight As, my dad would say, 'That's pretty good, but you can do better next semester.' There was an attitude of excellence when it came to me," Logan said. "It was about doing as good as you can and pushing yourself to a higher level."

As a teenager, Logan felt burdened by these expectations, and just couldn't understand why his dad was "such a ballbuster." But as an adult, he now understands that these high expectations were a key element in defining who he became as an adult. "My dad, more than anyone, made me who I am," Logan says. "He pushed me so hard because he believed I was capable of great things, and that belief in me had such a positive impact on my self-esteem. At the time, I didn't understand that, and I certainly didn't appreciate it." But he now sees this constant encouragement to strive as the very reason he is so successful and happy as an adult. "I'm internally driven. I measure myself against myself because of how I was raised," he explained. "It set my attitude to excellence and made me push myself to a higher level, even as an adult."

If only parents could visit the future and hear the gratitude their children eventually express, it would make being tough in the moment much more bearable.

When kids have regrets

Jack, from Phoenix, and his younger sister wish their parents had been more specific about locking on to a goal and striving for it. "My dad told me to explore, find the thing you love," Jack said. "There never was the component of working at it. I wish my parents had said aim your arrow at what you want and then point and shoot. I have the conviction that when and if I have children, I'm going to encourage them to pursue something diligently as opposed to an explore-the-world ethos." Jack wants to be more directive with his own children about setting their sights high and striving toward those lofty goals.

Sometimes kids are happy to get their parents' help in the moment, only to regret it later. When Sarah was in high school in New Orleans, she would procrastinate about writing papers because she knew that her mother would sit there with her and help her get them done at the last minute. In retrospect, she believes she might have taken more responsibility for her work in high school and been more invested in college if she had been expected to complete her work on her own. Instead, it took her longer to mature and realize her own capabilities.

Bill, the young photographer from Chicago, eventually decided that a career in the creative arts was not for him and chose to follow in his father's footsteps by going into the retail industry. He was delighted when his father hired him right out of college to work as a manager in his biggest store in downtown Chicago where, years earlier, his photographs had hung. But the experience was difficult for Bill. He came to believe it had been a huge mistake for his father to give him that job. "I was treated too much like family and not enough as an employee," he said. "To be treated from day one as a family member and as an owner, having my dad's last name as I walked in on my first day at the job—that was very different than if I'd walked into somewhere else." Ultimately, he felt this hindered him and took a toll on his self-confidence. "If your dad is giving you a job, how do you really know what you could have been elsewhere? I didn't prove myself to *myself*."

Now in his early 50's and head of his family's retail empire, he's instituted a policy that family members have to work outside the business and make a name for themselves before they can join the family business.

LOOKING TO THE FUTURE

Parenting is a monumental challenge in almost any circumstances, especially since there are no hard and fast rules. Since parents cannot look ahead and see how their actions will actually play out, it is often difficult to know in the moment whether their decisions are right or wrong. But having spoken to this intriguing and diverse group of inheritors—each of whom is successful in his or her own unique way—we had the opportunity to see how their parents' actions impacted them. And what we saw were children who grew up in phenomenal wealth and developed the necessary traits to become balanced, healthy, and happy adults.

"The self is born in the crucible of interaction between parent and child," writes Dr. Levine in her book *The Price of Privilege*. "Every time we encourage exploration, applaud independence, and require self-control we help our children grow into their best selves."[26] Perhaps the inheritors we interviewed here can teach others how to find the right balance in this critical relationship between parent and child, so that when it's time for the child to leave the nest and create his or her own future, that future looks bright.

....

CHAPTER THREE

Here's What We Think: Communicating Values

It's become increasingly common to impress upon wealthy families how critical it is to school their children in the nuts and bolts of financial literacy. Shelves are packed with how-to books on teaching kids to master money management; whether through establishing their own bank accounts, learning how to budget, managing and paying for personal credit cards, or joining investment clubs—entire industries have sprung up to address this basic need. And while this is certainly not a flawed approach, it proves to be a bit of a red herring.

Learning about money management at an early age is not the panacea many hope it to be. Our interviews of successful inheritors revealed a startling fact: Very few had received a textbook education in financial literacy. Rather, they learned by watching their parents: how they lived, what they talked about, what they valued, and what they didn't value. Those who were not taught explicit financial lessons at home developed a keen understanding of, and respect for, money as a result of absorbing the values their parents expressed, and a number were motivated by their solid grounding in money values to educate themselves in the nuts and bolts of financial literacy.

In an ideal world, affluent children would learn fundamentals about money values as well as receive a comprehensive financial education. However, if you could pick only one area of focus, it's the values that are far more important than the nuts and bolts. And, conversely, the nuts and bolts in absence of values—or worse, in contrast to them—are meaningless. This is why advisors brought in to provide financial literacy training to struggling young adults can hope to achieve only modest success. It's the difference between taking a continuing education course in Spanish versus being raised in a bilingual household.

Surprisingly, a recent survey[27] of high school students who took financial management classes in school revealed that they were no better off as young adults in terms of handling their money than students who did not take the classes. This supports the idea that consistently seeing financial literacy in action is far more effective and has greater impact than learning about it in the abstract.

Hurdles to overcome

If the most critical step parents can take to teach sound financial values to their children is to live those values themselves, then why doesn't this happen more often? What gets in the way?

Knowing how you feel about money, whether you've earned it or inherited it, and how to deal with it gracefully and sensibly is not a given. In families where wealth is newly acquired, it can take a high degree of attention, time, and introspection on the part of the parents to sort out their own conflicted feelings about wealth, values, and identity before they can hope to pass on any solid values to their children.

Parents who find themselves raising children in a setting more affluent than their own upbringing can find themselves unmoored amid the almost daily barrage of choices that reflect their socioeconomic identity: Private or public school for the children? First class or not? Comparison shopping or buying the first one you see? Almost every decision of daily life can stir deep internal conflicts about who the parent really is at his or her core. Regardless of whether the money has been inherited or earned, children pick up on this confusion and the inconsistency that it breeds.

The parents who were most successful in raising grounded children were those who felt comfortable with their own value system around consumption and money management and whose wealth did not change who they were at their core. Yet it also is often difficult for spouses to be on the same page. They may have had different money upbringings or developed different attitudes toward childrearing. But we learned that, without fail, the most successful parents operated as a team. In situations where they don't, children are confused at best and manipulative at worst.

Ultimately, the evidence is clear: Having parents who modeled the financial behavior they wanted their children to adopt, and who did so consistently and as a team, was a critical component of how our inheritors launched on the right foot. Let these stories be a road map for how you might achieve this in your own family.

ESTABLISHING SOUND MONEY VALUES

Our interviews teemed with rich stories of parents who had consistent money values and articulated and modeled them regularly. The following messages seemed to have the most positive and lasting effect on our successful inheritors.

Value #1: Material Possessions Aren't That Important

Henry spent his youth doing all the kinds of activities that kids growing up with old money typically do. His home in the New York suburbs was built in 1820 and included stables, a gardener's cottage, and a full-sized greenhouse. He attended a well-known elite boarding school for which he had to wear a blazer and a tie. His parents went into the city frequently to attend fundraising galas at the Met and the Ballet. "We were visible people in society," he said.

Yet growing up, Henry never had the sense that his parents particularly cared about money because they never spent much of it on themselves. He described his father as a classic old Wasp who delighted in a good deal. "He was a dapper dresser. He always looked good, but he never believed in the showy things," Henry said. He recalls his father showing off a pair of shoes he had bought for a low price, saying with pride, "They look pretty good, don't they?" He would pull into the Westchester Country Club lot, filled with gleaming Mercedes, driving "an awful old Buick."

The main financial message Henry's parents passed on to him was: "Don't screw up the nest egg." They taught him that families like theirs should never sell principal; everyone should live off income, containing habits and expenses so that they can live within the boundaries of whatever that income is. As a result, Henry and his three siblings live within their means—and even today, not one of them drives a showy car.

In exploring the stark contrast between how his parents raised him and what he sees now living in the neighboring town from where he grew up, Henry reflected on what he called a "shift around the axis of ego." By this he meant a societal shift over the last 30 years toward a more ostentatious way of life. His parent's generation strove to be Spartan and the very last thing they wanted to do was show off wealth. Their attitude was, in Henry's words, "For God's sake, if the oven isn't broken, let's not get another one." Yet nowadays, people's attitudes have shifted and their thinking is more along the lines of "I deserve the highest level of comfort I can afford." This can be seen at play in today's kitchen, which used to be the smallest and most modest room in the house and is now a vast cockpit of family life. Everyone feels compelled to have the latest cool-looking new model oven or flatscreen TV over their custom-built cabinets. "People have lost their gyroscope," Henry mused, "and in this move toward greater personal consumption, people are often not considering the effect this may have on their children's attitudes."

With his own children, Henry models frugal behavior just as his parents did, and teaches them that money and possessions are not what matter most in life. "Most of what we're imparting on them is by showing them how we live," he said.

Keeping priorities straight

David grew up as the oldest of three just outside San Francisco (his sister is Eve, whom we met earlier), not far from the beaches overlooking the city where people sailed the harbor and swam when the weather was good. Along his street most families had beautiful backyard pools, many of them with their own cabanas and hot tubs as well as elaborate landscaping. But even though his parents could have easily afforded to put in a pool, when David asked them why they didn't have one, their answer was a lesson in restraint. "We don't need a pool," his father said. "The beach is just down the block!"

Highlighting the concept of need versus desire helped set up the children in his family for a healthy personal relationship with money. In addition, David was learning about the gap between appearances and reality. His parents pointed out that just because a neighbor drove a Lexus did not mean that he had money, as he could have gone into debt to acquire it. "They told us very early on that material things may or may not mean that a person has wealth," David said. "What you see is not always what you get. I learned the notion of debt and credit. We were reflecting on the materialistic aspect of money and introducing the concept of choice."

Perhaps the most important lesson David and his siblings absorbed growing up was that their parents were not invested in what the neighbors thought of them, in spite of living in an environment where many people were trying to keep up with the Joneses. "They didn't make financial decisions in order to fit in," he explained. "They made decisions to better us and give us opportunities."

Among our interviewees, the levels of wealth a family enjoyed did not always correlate with their spending patterns: Even those families that did not need to exercise any financial restraint showed moderation where spending was concerned. The young publishing executive Sam, for instance, often had conversations with her parents about what was really worth spending money on. Frequently, her father used these talks to highlight a specific value around money. She recalls him telling her once when they were talking about flying in a private plane: "Why would you waste $5,000 to fly a plane when you could give $5,000 to a local school to help a kid?"

Putting expenditures into perspective in this way helped our inheritors develop sound money values early on, which they then carried through to adulthood.

Value #2: Money Has Its Place

Taylor grew up in Atlanta with a twin brother, enjoying life in an old mansion in the Buckhead district. Her parents taught her that while money had its place, it was not central to their lives.

While their wealth afforded them opportunities and luxuries other families might not be able to enjoy, they did not choose to spend liberally across the board. One of the family's priorities, for example, was adventure travel. They loved the time together, and wanted to show their children the broader world. One year they went to Africa, the next to France. They rented a sailboat for a tour around Greece and hiked through the Lake District in England. While Taylor remembers these trips as exotic and exciting, she also noted that they always flew coach and she and her brother sometimes even shared hotel rooms with her parents. When they went out to eat, they would eat in regular local establishments, and often took along picnics for daytime eating. The focus was more on togetherness and less on the luxuries.

Now raising her own children, ages six and four, Taylor consciously impresses on them what really matters in life. When her kids are crying for something they want, she says, "Why are you crying? You have everything you could ever need—you have parents who love you, and grandparents who love you!"

It was clear that her parents valued human connections over external criteria, and Taylor has absorbed this as a basic tenet of her own parenting style.

Family and character are more important than money

During the summers and most holiday weekends, Henry (from New York) spent time on his grandmother's property near the Bush compound in Kennebunkport, Maine. His family would play on the beach, gather in the Great Room to play cards and charades, and in the mornings, watch his grandmother cook huge breakfasts in the kitchen. Though she had a butler and a chauffeur, his grandmother loved to put on her apron and fry eggs or pancakes for the extended family rather than hire a cook to do it. The focus was on family: "The money didn't seem that important," Henry said. "When we were together we talked a lot about cousins and relatives."

At the time, he wondered about the inconsistencies in spending he was witnessing and asked his grandmother why she didn't just get a cook to make the breakfast. She waved him away, explaining that she loved her time with the family too much to let someone else take over the cooking. "I learned early on that money doesn't make people happy," Henry said, "family and friends do. We had no pretensions about wealth or being a big dog."

In particular, Henry learned that ultimately it's not the trappings of wealth that draw people into the fold, but the lure of an individual's personality. His mother Katharine, for example, was not the most ostentatious hostess but her ebullient personality was like a magnet. "She was a lousy cook, but everyone liked being in my house because my mother was so entertaining," he said. "It taught me the values of family, connection, fun." His mother valued creating meaningful human connections over displays of privilege or social clout. "If she went to a house to play bridge and Ronald Reagan was there," Henry explained, "she wouldn't come home and say, 'Oh we met Ronald Reagan.' She'd say, 'Oh we had a great bridge game; we laughed and laughed. . . . '"

Value #3: How to Spend: Saving Up for Value and Quality

When there's plenty of money in the bank, the temptation to buy now and forego saving up for purchases is often irresistible. But families that model saving and encourage their children to save are helping their children to develop character traits that will serve them well for the rest of their financial lives. They learn about self-control, delayed gratification, appreciation, and the real value of a dollar.

As a child, Taylor remembers hearing anecdotes about how her parents saved for her education when they were younger; they told her, "We can afford to send you to private school because we saved early in our marriage. We went out to dinner only once a week to the Chinese restaurant."

Taylor's mother continued to model the value of saving and having a specific goal as Taylor grew. Though she could have afforded anything she might have wanted, she loved to scour the sales racks at various department stores and get good value for money. She would advise her daughter to shop at the end of the season so she could get clothes for the following season at an incredible discount. Watching how carefully her mother spent money and how much she enjoyed getting a good deal impressed on Taylor that money wasn't to be treated with a cavalier attitude just because she had a lot of it. Over the years she internalized this message: *It's better to wait and save to buy something of quality that's going to last longer.*

Logan, whose father was by nature an avid saver, not only taught his son about the satisfaction of saving for and buying something on his own, but also emphasized to him that when earning money he should pay himself before paying the bills. At age 10 or 11, Logan spent hours leafing though an enormous Service Merchandise catalogue looking for his first adult watch, which he planned to buy with his own money. After several months, he had saved up $150 by working and he was able to buy himself the watch he had been eyeing. To this day he remembers fondly the experience of saving for a long time to get something he wanted. "The anticipation of buying something is so gratifying," Logan explained. "As I got wealthier I've discovered it's less satisfying to just buy yourself what you want than if you have to wait. You get the enjoyment of the object but not of the journey."

In learning that instant gratification does not confer a lasting sense of satisfaction, wealthy kids begin to understand that focusing on deeper motivations—like developing a sense of purpose and building a community of friends—lead to healthier outcomes in the long run.

TAKING IT A STEP FURTHER: SHOW, DON'T TELL

Talking publically about money is considered gauche. This taboo on discussing finances is even more prevalent in affluent families. The reasons for this reluctance are understandable: parents are concerned that in discussing money they are opening a can of worms and inviting questions they may not want to answer.

Yet, unless families of means model real-life experiences to their children about how they deal with money issues, how will these young people learn to navigate the financial world once they're on their own? There's no avoiding the fact that at some point in their lives, inheritors have to make both short- and long-term decisions that involve money matters. Having a clear set of principles that have been modeled to them consistently throughout their childhood gives them a solid basis from which to form their own opinions.

Better even than sitting down and having a money talk or hiring an advisor to teach financial literacy is showing children through your behavior how to deal with money on a day-to-day basis.

Just because we have it, doesn't mean we have to spend it

As we discovered in our interviews, parents who showed through their behavior how they dealt with money issues and budgeting helped their children get a leg up when it came to managing their own finances after college and into adult life. Sharing the reality of negotiating one's financial life, even when it's not glamorous, takes away some of the mystery and confusion that can otherwise cloud a young adult's judgment.

After marrying, David's parents launched a family business that they grew for six years before it was bought by an international food conglomerate. When he was little, his family lived in a large, custom-built home outside San Francisco and enjoyed substantial luxury. Yet David vividly remembers spending time with his father in his home office on Sundays while his dad outlined the family's weekly budget on Quicken. They were both early risers, and it was during those quiet morning hours that he was able to observe his father.

"I spent years with him while he was doing the bills. I love those memories. It was extra time I got with my dad because he was working all day," David said. "I learned from that how important it is to have a budget, to know where every dollar is spent." And rather than having to endure a finger-wagging lecture, he was able to enjoy the gift of one-on-one time with a busy parent.

Even though the family did not need to worry about being able to pay the bills, they nonetheless continued to manage their money the way they had before they came into wealth. Whenever his father got a large bonus, the family would institute a spending freeze as a way of ensuring that they didn't spend the extra money right away but were thoughtful about how they were planning to use it.

His sister, Eve, remembers not being allowed to rent a video because they were on "lock down" mode—her mother would tell her to go read a book instead. But rather than seeing this as a hardship, she recalls it with humor. These restrictions taught the children that they could survive if and when they had to cut back, and that they didn't need money or possessions to keep them occupied. "It was a check into reality," said David. "We don't have to live extravagantly just because we have all this money."

Learning by doing

Remember Bill, whose father owned the department stores? When Bill was 16, his dad decided to buy a new car and bring his son along for the negotiations. They drove over to the auto mile outside Chicago and headed for the dealership. The whole process "bored me to tears," Bill said, and seemed to drag on all day long. He would far rather have been hanging out with his friends at the local park. But the take away for Bill was that you "don't give away hard-earned money without making sure you're getting great value." The lessons were far more effective because of his experience of actually sitting through the discussions rather than just hearing about them later.

Not only that, but Bill saw the art of negotiation in action. As he endured the endless back and forth between the two men, he saw his father making the time to ensure he was getting a fair shake. ("I also learned you don't negotiate with a salesman; always negotiate with the sales manager!" he added.) When to stand your ground and when to be flexible is an important lesson for inheritors to learn. However tangentially, observing this interplay also helped Bill later in life by teaching him that regardless of how much money you have, you never want to allow yourself to be taken advantage of.

This message about being in control of the money rather than allowing it to control you is important for children who might otherwise grow up believing that because money is plentiful, they needn't bother paying close attention to how it is spent. At tax time, Bill watched his father doing his own returns. "He was sitting on the floor of his bedroom surrounded by tax documents," Bill said. While he learned the lesson that his dad was "saving money by doing it on his own," even more impressive was "the incredible detail with which he had to familiarize himself in order to file the returns." Now in charge of this retail empire, Bill likens this thoroughness and insistence on being in control to the way he prepares for an important business meeting. He learned by watching his father in action and he uses these skills daily.

Showing them how it's done

Sometimes drawing the curtain aside and showing children how to manage everyday tasks like paying bills and reconciling budgets is just what's needed in order to help them put money in the right perspective. As we've seen, many inheritors spoke of watching their parents pay bills and getting a glimpse of the inner workings of a household budget—but some said their parents had taken this a step further.

When Matteo was growing up in an affluent family in India, he had friends who got more money per day to spend than he got in a year. Surrounded by children of affluence who spent money indiscriminately, Matteo in contrast developed a keen sense of the value of money and the mechanics of paying for things. Each Saturday, he sat down in the breakfast room with his father and went over an "expense report" for the week—he called it "a device to enable a conversation." In that report, Matteo had to list everything he'd bought, whether it was textbooks or pencils.

"It was father and son time," he said. "This guaranteed us a couple of hours when there was an exchange of thought and direction which was carried on through later life." His father acted as mentor, coach, and sounding board as they talked about the week and the various experiences Matteo had had. This led to a closeness that continued even when Matteo left India for the United States.

In a notebook, Matteo recorded his purchases on one side of the page and stapled receipts on the other. "My father never commented on my individual spending decisions," he said. "There was more of an overarching theme of not spending frivolously and being held accountable for knowing how the money was spent and how much was left over. It was an important message to me—it was accountability mixed with a message of trust." Matteo learned about being held responsible for his actions, and his father demonstrated that he respected his son's decisions.

Sam's mother, from Houston, makes binders for each of her kids in which she puts their bank statements so they can talk about where the money is going. "She doesn't stalk what we're doing," Sam said, "but she's monitoring." She's smart about when she makes comments, sometimes going for months without saying something and then gently prodding with a "Have you realized you are running low?" or jumping in to correct her daughter's behavior by saying, "You just can't spend money on that!" or, "You can't be this person!"

Sam appreciates that her parents are paying attention.

"They seem like they're looking out for us, not like they're lecturing us," she explained. "They're not oblivious people; they're not just giving out money and not caring where it's going."

Our interviews revealed a pattern: The most successful parents were able to achieve a balance between holding their children accountable and conveying a sense of trust in their children and respect for their decisions. This was far easier when parents lived congruently with the values they were attempting to teach, literally showing their children how to behave and what was expected of them.

As we will see, another effective communication tool that will help children become grounded adults is achieved by giving them a foundational understanding of family stories.

CREATE CONTEXT BY TELLING STORIES

Some years ago, Emory University conducted a study[28] analyzing how children are impacted by talking with their parents about their family history. The first part of the research was undertaken in mid-2001 and the results showed that the children who knew more about their family's history had a stronger sense of control over their lives, as well as higher self-esteem and a stronger belief in the health of their families. Two months later, the researchers surveyed the same group of children again, but this time after the trauma of 9/11. This second sample confirmed that those children who knew more about their families were more resilient and could better handle the effects of stress. It was a resounding confirmation of the researchers' initial theories about the importance of sharing family stories.

"Through narrative interactions about shared past, parents help children's understanding of who they were, who they are now, and presumably who they will be in the future, both as individuals and as members of the family," they wrote. "Thus, though family communications and interaction in other contexts and settings is clearly important, the role of family narratives may be particularly critical for children's developing sense of self."[29]

We found that sharing both the good and the bad stories helps wealthy children put their financial position in context and shapes their understanding of their privilege in a way that underscores key messages. In particular, understanding family ups and downs seemed to help our inheritors in two specific ways: by allowing them to internalize the notion of impermanence, and by encouraging a sense of perspective and gratitude.

Understanding the idea of scarcity

As a child growing up in a spacious prewar apartment in the West Village, Craig, whom we met early in chapter 1, had a keen understanding of his parents' histories. They had lived through World War II and the Holocaust, and before that his grandparents had survived the Depression. "They somehow transmitted some sense of fear that things could go wrong," Craig explained. "Culturally, we knew about the Holocaust pulling the carpet out from under your feet." They communicated a palpable sense that "we have a lot but could always lose it all. Things could go terribly wrong."

As a result, Craig and his older sister had no sense of entitlement, but rather understood the concept of scarcity. This is a concept that many high net worth families were forced to face head on during the economic crash of 2008 when their portfolios shrank. But rather than waiting for external forces to determine when and how you handle such a crisis, it's far better and healthier to be prepared in advance.

The idea that the wealth is neither endless nor necessarily permanent actually helps young people understand that they should be prepared to survive under any financial circumstance if they want to feel secure financially and emotionally.

Over the years growing up in Rockport, Massachusetts, Ross had also heard many stories about the ebb and flow of his family's fortunes. As the Emory researchers noted, the most helpful stories to share with children are "the oscillating family narratives," which are the kind of stories Ross heard from his parents. These oscillating narratives tell of both the wild successes a family enjoys and the heartbreaking struggles. They teach children that people can learn to survive anything as long as they have resilience, foresight, and a support system.

Both of Ross's parents came from old money that grew and shrank over the generations depending on historical circumstances, family choices, and individual malfeasance. On his father's side the money ran out because his great grandparents and great-great grandparents were philanthropists and gave most of it away. His grandfather was a lawyer who didn't care about money and did not bill his clients during the Depression. Growing up, his mother heard the stories from her side of the family about relatives who misappropriated money leaving them all with less than before.

Knowing the financial triumphs and woes of several generations before him helped Ross absorb the notion that the family money could run out. Seeing examples of the shirtsleeves-to-shirtsleeves phenomena in his own family, "taught me to live within my means, and that my means were good but not great," he said.

Cultivating gratitude

The majority of our interviewees had a palpable (and unusual, from the perspective of the wealth management industry) sense that the money was their parent's money, not theirs, and felt genuinely grateful for the money that their parents had chosen to share with them. This is a welcome antidote to the stereotypical picture of the mercenary, entitled young beneficiary for whom no amount of wealth transfer is enough. How did our interviewees' parents cultivate this sense of gratitude?

The inheritors' thankfulness for the money they were able to enjoy seems to have grown from the way the parents communicated about that money with them. Parents frequently and intentionally pointed out to their children while they were growing up that they should be appreciative of all they had. They contrasted kids' experiences with their own upbringing, or at least talked about their own upbringing and how they came from less. They were honest about the world and that others had less than they did. In not sheltering them, they helped the children have more appreciation for what they had.

Sam remembers hearing stories about her father arriving in the United States and getting his first job. "My dad's background really affects how I look at life. He came here with absolutely nothing," she said. "It's an American dream story that you don't see a lot anymore. Because of this, my parents were keenly aware of the benefits of what we were enjoying and wanted to make sure we were too. They never just gave us something. It was always in the context of, 'You should really appreciate this. This isn't something every kid gets. You have to work for this.'"

She understood that the advantages she enjoyed were not the norm; other children did not necessarily enjoy such abundance. When they traveled over Christmas to exotic island locales, her parents would point out, "It isn't casual to go on this trip—it's not something that every family gets to do."

Sam's biggest fear was disappointing her parents. "Because they had always done so much for us," she said, "and given us all these opportunities. I knew how they grew up and how they had all these struggles. I wanted to make them proud."

Mark, who moved from Washington, D.C., to New York as a teenager, vividly recalled how grateful he felt to his dad for using his contacts to help him get the right sort of professional experiences through college. He and his brother "felt even more responsible because we got that help and had that advantage. Whatever we got, we appreciated and didn't take it for granted. We didn't have the right not to take it seriously," he explained. "We understood that we were lucky, we were special, we were fortunate."

Launching his career, Mark always felt his parents would help him if he needed it. "There was a backstop, but I never wanted to take it," he said. In fact, Mark's gratitude increased his determination to work hard and make them proud. It became his goal to pay them back for all the guidance and support they'd given him over the years. "I made it a personal mission to hold up my end of the bargain and pay them back for what they've done for me," he said. Now raising children of his own, Mark said, "Whatever I got from my parents isn't mine. I want to pay it forward and I want to do in my own life for my children what my parents did for me."

Let them know what you think

In the moment, it may not appear that children are absorbing or appreciating what parents say and do when it comes to money—or anything else, for that matter. But what we heard consistently over dozens of interviews was that when reflecting on their upbringing, inheritors were heavily influenced by their parents' opinions and actions. It's critically important for wealthy parents to work through and articulate thoughts about money values for themselves, and align themselves with their spouses, so they can proactively find opportunities to model these behaviors for their children.

Every action has a consequence, and the kids are watching. Pablo Picasso once said, "I'd like to live as a poor man with lots of money." In many ways, this is a core message we heard repeated again and again: There's far more to life than money.

Ultimately, it's the values you share about the use of money—and the values you actively model—that will have a lasting effect and will enable your children to become grateful, grounded adults who see their wealth with a healthy perspective.

....

CHAPTER FOUR

Get a Real Job: Why Working Is Key

For children of the very wealthy, figuring out what to do with their lives is often one of the most significant challenges they face. While they may not have to work to put food on the table, they do have to find a calling that makes them feel useful and relevant, keeps them connected with the world, and allows them to continue to grow and learn throughout their lives. Most people don't aspire to being rich, aimless, and bored.

Daniel Pink, author of books about the changing nature of work, has written that people used to think of work as a "disutility," which means that they would avoid it if they didn't get paid. Now he argues it can be thought of as a "utility," meaning people do it for no immediate return. They work because it gives their lives a sense of purpose.

Two researchers studying issues of motivation at the University of Rochester, Edward Deci and Richard Ryan, coined the term *self-determination theory*, which emphasizes the role autonomy plays in achieving life satisfaction, and also identifies competence and relatedness (human connection) as additional emotional needs. These three needs are greatly enhanced when we experience satisfying work lives. As Ross, one of our inheritors from Massachusetts said, "I'm 68 and I can't imagine retiring—it makes me nervous. What would I do with my brain?"

Working enables young people to separate from their parents emotionally and financially, which is critical to their successful launch into adulthood. Maintaining a job requires resilience, time investment, flexibility, conscientiousness, humility, and creativity. It's hard work to train for a job, seek a job, keep that job and, once you have it, turn it into a career. So the ultimate question for affluent parents is: *How do we instill the desire to work—and the will to work through tough times—in children who don't need to work for money?*

The correlation between work and happiness

Over decades of studying happiness, researchers Martin Seligman and Christopher Peterson made two important findings that are relevant to our discussion: First, they identified 24 character strengths that are proven to positively impact life satisfaction and success, and second, they determined that those traits can be learned, practiced, and taught. In his book *How Children Succeed*, journalist Paul Tough narrows these 24 strengths down to seven critical traits: zest, optimism, curiosity, self-control, social intelligence, gratitude, and grit. He explains that character, as Seligman defines it, is not about morality, but about "learning a set of skills to help children achieve their goals."[30] In studying our inheritors and their experiences with work—both in the home as youngsters and outside the home later in life—it became apparent that there was an important connection between their own development of these seven character traits and their extensive and varied work lives.

"Wealthy kids don't have to bust their asses to find the thing that will make them money, and so they have to find what makes them happy," explained Peter, a writer in his mid-30's who provides promotional copy for studios out in L.A. "Obviously that's a beautiful thing to be able to do, but the fact is, it's also incredibly stressful."

Introspective and determined, Peter struggled to find work in the creative world early in his career, and relied on supplements from his family's money to see him through lean times in the business. Being dependent in this way was profoundly uncomfortable for him, and he spent many years in therapy trying to untangle his relationship between making money, spending it, and using family money—and figuring out what it all meant in terms of love and life satisfaction. "There's the perception that you [affluent kids] should have a lead in figuring this out. It [money] makes procrastination a whole lot easier; it makes being distracted a whole lot harder to fight against because you don't have that hunger," he said. "You just have to find it from within yourself."

Wealthy parents can help children find and use this hunger. When parents encourage children to experience the joys and inevitable aggravations of working, they are helping them learn fundamental lessons that are difficult for them to learn in any other way. As we discussed earlier, children need to experience challenge in order to grow. "Only through freely chosen discipline can life be enjoyed and still kept within the bounds of reason," wrote research psychologist Mihaly Csikszentmihalyi, a scholar of the concept of flow. Flow is a desirable mental state during which you are immersed in a feeling of energized focus, involvement, and enjoyment of process—and Csikszentmihalyi stressed, "The prerequisite for happiness is the ability to get fully involved in life."[31] As another of our interviewees, Gaby, said about her time-consuming but satisfying job as the head of a university press, "I want to be part of conversations that are interesting. I want to be on the move." People yearn to feel "flow," and to be able to experience that, they must first understand the principles of work, motivation, and satisfaction.

Yet, wealthy parents often unintentionally underestimate the importance of work, inhibiting their children from developing important traits that contribute significantly to their future happiness. Wealthy parents often don't realize how their financial involvement in their children's lives can remove the incentive to work, at a critical time when incentive is just what is needed to motivate the child to engage in the work world. It is through that very engagement that the child ultimately derives contentment, satisfaction, self-pride, and confidence.

However, financial necessity is a far stronger motivation than the amorphous promise of future contentment. Often, parents make it possible financially for their children to sidestep the working world in ways that less fortunate kids could never afford to do, unwittingly depriving their children of invaluable life experiences.

It is unfortunately quite common that money inherited from or given by parents which is designed to be only a "safety net" actually serves as a parachute to nowhere. Young adults end up using this money to flit from one thing to the next or to walk away from a job just when the going gets tough. This robs them of the chance to push through difficult times and develop a clear sense of purpose, and work toward building a career. All too often, they look around at age 30 and their CV pales in comparison to their friends' who didn't have the same "advantages."

Frequently, wealthy parents discourage their kids from working in high school in favor of other enrichment experiences such as travel or volunteering, believing that these are just as valuable, if not more valuable (and certainly more fun) than working in the local mall or at a restaurant. Eve, the TV producer we met earlier, is expecting her first child. When she looks around her at the parenting practices in L.A. where she now lives, she's not convinced they serve the children well. Her experience growing up included volunteering in soup kitchens and working numerous jobs as a babysitter, waitress, and cashier. "Now I see parents giving their children opportunities and saying 'You can work later,'" she says, "but for me to make minimum wage and work with people who live off minimum wage salaries was eye-opening."

IT ALL STARTS SMALL, AND IN YOUR OWN HOME

One key to being capable of launching and maintaining a satisfying work life is developing the trait of conscientiousness. This is manifested in efficient, organized, and systematic behaviors, and it includes such elements as self-discipline, attention to detail, and the ability to think carefully before acting, as well as the desire and need for achievement.

Conscientiousness does not necessarily come naturally to humans, but the good news is that it can be developed and practiced. When parents maintain high expectations about their children's sense of responsibility around the house and hold them to these expectations, it allows those children to have daily practice in pushing through unpleasant or boring activities they would otherwise never choose to engage in. Doing these activities then becomes a habit, which in turn makes completing them less unpleasant and more satisfying. The mental training of disciplining themselves to attend to their responsibilities stays with children and becomes internalized as part of their work ethic.

As a boy, Peter, who works for the studios in L.A., was expected to keep his room tidy. "It's about responsibility, really; that's what it comes down to," he said. "It's onerous, these responsibilities, those kinds of everyday chores that feel too vague and too annoying unless they're turned into habits. But it's a *tool* to develop the tolerance of doing something you don't want to do."

Most parents know that getting children to do chores around the house is a good way to teach them about conscientiousness, yet few American parents have the energy to insist on their children completing household work—it simply takes too much organization and vigilance. Doing well in academics is often the "work" expected of our children. Yet among the inheritors we interviewed, memories of their parents having high expectations of their "citizenship" in the house reminded us how important it is to build toward a good work ethic by learning to work at home.

Growing up a twin in the South, Taylor recalls her parents holding her and her brother to high standards. They had to make their own beds, set the table for dinner, pick up their toys, keep their rooms neat, and take good care of their own things. They were expected to be "good citizens around the house." Her brother, Scott, also remembered his parents telling him, "Don't come down to breakfast before you've made your bed." As he explained, "Cleaning up your room was your *job* in the house."

Matteo, whom we met earlier, is from northern India. When he was young, his parents employed numerous servants to help run the household; they had three live-in staff and two chauffeurs. Yet the parents had three nonnegotiable expectations for their boys: The first was that the boys would set and clear the table every day; this was a ritual that became an important part of the quality time the family spent together. The second was that they kept their rooms tidy, including making their own beds. And the third, and perhaps most impactful expectation was that the boys make their own way to their sports activities even though the family employed chauffeurs. They took the bus or rode their bikes, even if it meant getting up an hour earlier. "The work ethic was very strong in our family," Matteo said. "It's how you give back, whether you get paid or not."

While to some it might seem odd—and certainly inconvenient—to expect young boys to spend time getting from one point to another when they could easily be driven, the lesson they learned was one of self-reliance. For suburban Americans, this might not seem a reasonable expectation of children, but for Matteo it taught him early on that he had nonnegotiable responsibilities. This later fueled his self-belief, giving him the confidence that he could break free of the family's shadow and make something of his own life, independently.

Children naturally have poorly developed impulse control, lack judgment, and are self-involved—and nonetheless, parents often expect them to absorb basic elements of self-care and home management through osmosis rather than practice. Instead, it helps them in the long run to begin instilling a work ethic in the home by getting them to pitch in on a regular basis, and holding them accountable when they don't do their part. This helps them develop two of the seven character traits outlined earlier by journalist Paul Tough: grit (a combination of drive and perseverance) and self-control.

As child's first employers, parents set the standards

As a ten-year-old in Mill Valley, California, Kent started mowing the lawn once a week for his parents. They had a sizable backyard with lush grass that ended in a small stream at the edge of their property. It took Kent almost two hours to complete the mowing, and when he was done his father would inspect his work before declaring whether it passed muster or not. He frequently washed his father's car and if he missed a spot he'd be expected to wash the entire car again. "I learned it's easier to do it right the first time," Kent said. "There was incredible attention to detail." Kent also learned the value of money: for each chore well done, he earned $5. When it wasn't done to his father's satisfaction, he earned nothing.

While this may seem draconian to some, Kent credits it with shaping his attitude toward excellence. "It made me push myself," he said, "and showed me what I was capable of." Now that he has his own children, he makes sure they do chores and earn money so that they buy items like video games and toys from their own savings.

He also feels that his father's tough attitude toward work and responsibilities played a pivotal role in helping him become an organized, focused, and resilient leader. In his current role at the helm of the start-up business he founded a decade ago, Kent is empowered to make calculated decisions and hold others to high standards, contributing to the growth of his enterprise.

Eve explained how it worked in her family growing up: "You didn't get money for free." As with Kent, Eve's brother David remembers only getting paid when he'd done his chores "the right way." Not only this, but Eve and her siblings were not given the choice whether to help or not; they were expected to pitch in. "Your responsibilities were not optional," she said. "You had your job, you were told to do it. You weren't going to not do it." They were all required to do chores in order to get their weekly allowance. Their parents felt that when they "employed" their children around the house, they were standing in for the employers who would follow later in life.

In respect to household responsibilities, one sticking point in current parenting literature is whether or not it's wise to pay children for completing chores. While most of our interviewees were not paid for their at-home work, some were. The prevailing wisdom is that you should not link allowances to household jobs because certain responsibilities should be required without payment. And there is the additional concern that paying children to do chores gives them a bargaining chip: They can refuse to do their chores if they don't need the money.

However, in the stories we heard, *not* doing the work was never presented as an option. Kids were expected to complete the task *and* they were paid only when they did so. What the parents expected from their children was the important issue; there was no room for bargaining. They held their children to high standards and expected them to complete their work. When money was involved in the transaction—and this was more the case with ad hoc family chores like washing the car than with personal responsibilities like making your bed—the lessons learned by the children were positive. The payment acted as an incentive that motivated the children not only to do what was asked of them, but also to do it well. They remembered their chores with surprising fondness, and attributed doing them to helping develop their proclivity for order and self-motivation as adults. And the ability to tie a job well done to economic remuneration set them up well for the adult financial world—both in the earning power it represented and the multiple lessons they learned stewarding the money they earned.

Parents are the ultimate role models

Daniel, from Boston, always knew when the cleaning woman was coming because his mother would start picking up the house before she arrived. "She didn't want the housekeeper to show up to a mess," he said. At the time he didn't understand her motivation, but he later came to realize that his mother took pride in maintaining her household and saw a certain level of order as a personal responsibility. It was clear as he got older that keeping her home attractive also made his mother happy.

When he was a teenager, his mother suffered from breast cancer and the doctors ordered her to rest after having a double mastectomy. Even during that time, his mother did light housework and made sure there were fresh flowers on the windowsill. She did not want to feel helpless, and so she continued doing the activities that gave her pleasure. She experienced joy from the process. Her son learned from her that some people are more at ease when they are constantly contributing meaningfully to their environment—whether that means family or work life. He absorbed this lesson into his own independent life, and now finds himself driven by a sense of diligence, responsibility, and pride.

Our parents are, in many ways, the ultimate role models of work ethic and conscientiousness. By letting us in on the ups and downs (and occasional tediousness) of work and responsibility, they help us understand how the world works. So too, for our wealthy inheritors, many of whom recounted story after story of their parents talking about work or doing work at home.

Mark, our interviewee who moved to New York City as a teenager, recalled how he and his brother recognized their parents' work ethic early on: "We saw that they had a sense of responsibility and moderation," he said. While his father often missed family dinner during the weekdays, he would tuck the kids in before they fell asleep at night. "We saw the work that it took him to achieve his success—the late nights, the hard work. We saw the value in what that work achieved."

Mark's father was a fascinating case study because not only did he model hard work to them, but he also shared work stories when he was with his children at home. He loved talking about the daily trials and successes of turning businesses around, working through the problems he was facing in the office, "fighting fires, coming up with solutions, talking basically all about problems and how he dealt with them." As they got older, he shared more and more details with his boys.

"We developed a hell of a lot of appreciation for the fact that he threw himself in it, subjected himself to chaos, challenge, high levels of aggravation. He was pushing himself and he wasn't doing it for the money. He was guided by a really, really strong work ethic," Mark said. "A sense of obligation to the companies and workers he was dealing with to make them better. A sense of high standards. As kids, we were internalizing those standards and holding them up for ourselves."

Mark also learned that, even more than talking about values, leading by example was what really left a lasting impression. "I think this idea that leading first and foremost by your actions and behaviors is important," he said.

Work is a way of life

As a young child, John was always observing people around him. Sensitive and astute, he eventually became an art dealer and gallery owner. Even though his work differs radically from the real estate business his father is involved in, John absorbed important lessons he learned from watching his father.

In his household, the mantra was "We work a lot; we are workers." On weekends, John recalls his father coming home with "a giant bag of work and somehow, miraculously, through the nights, the bag would be empty." The message this kind of constancy sends to children is internalized in ways that impact them forever. One especially important lesson they learn from experiences like this is about delayed gratification: You work first and play later.

Expecting immediate gratification can set children up to be disappointing to others and to be disappointed themselves, and yet so often parents unconsciously fuel the fire of their children's need for instant pleasure. Naturally, it's hard for parents to watch their children suffer, but it's also hard for them to observe their kids being impatient or getting frustrated, even if parents know how important it is for their kids to experience and get control over these feelings. Gaby spent a lot of time with her paternal grand-parents when she was growing up in northern Florida. She remembers her grandfather would always say, "There are a couple times in your life where you really need to work hard, and then you can relax a bit. If you put your time in, then you can enjoy yourself."

Harvard psychologist Harry Stybel studied ten affluent families in an effort to figure out why some of their children turned out well and others did not. In one interview, he spoke about Leo, the son of a policeman who won a scholarship to MIT and then created his own software company. Even though Leo worked extremely hard, each morning he drove his two young children to school. He used himself "as a role model to show the drama, excitement, and failure of business," wrote Stybel. "He made his business life something that children could grasp. Sometimes you win and sometimes you lose. And even if you lose, you recover and move on."[32] This message about weathering life's ups and downs, and trusting that with enough effort and perseverance you will likely prevail, helped his children develop resilience.

In socializing his children about both the fun and the grind of business, Leo was also debunking its mystery. His kids were able to grasp some of the realities of the work world and therefore felt more capable of, and less intimidated by, entering into that world themselves.

GETTING A JOB OUTSIDE THE HOUSE

It is not enough to simply talk about work, or even to model a good work ethic. Children need to experience the real world of work for themselves.

Among the inheritors we spoke with, a surprisingly large number started "working" outside the house at a very early age. Jack, the film editor, parked cars at an outdoor agricultural fair in Maine when he was only 11 years old. (Those were the days!) He remembers coveting the blue T-shirts the "big boys" got to wear when they worked for the fair. "There was a piece of me feeling like it was a step in the direction of adulthood," he said, "getting compensation, wearing the staff shirt." Gaby babysat for her neighbor's two children when she was 12. Henry brought in the trash from the houses on his street when he was just nine years old. And David started his own home-based computer consulting service at age 15. The sheer variety of starter jobs was extraordinary, including waiter/waitress, ice cream scooper, store cashier, mall worker, boat cleaner, assembly line worker, driver, trash collector, computer troubleshooter, baggage handler, video producer, and ESL teacher.

Without their parents setting the expectation of them getting a "real job," and making them believe they were capable of handling that responsibility, it would never have occurred to these wealthy kids to do so. Yet the joy of working—even when working in jobs that are not fulfilling—can be immensely motivating; even unrewarding work teaches lessons and helps hone a child's sense of self.

Setting the appropriate expectations

But how do parents go about setting these expectations? It boils down to a straightforward message, delivered consistently and intentionally. At some point, parents need to articulate this simple fact to their children: *You need to work.*

Even though Mark was a city kid, during summers he enjoyed time visiting his grandparents in Maine for a month or more. Then, the summer before he went to college, Mark's father told him that he would be working on the assembly line in one of his factories in New Jersey. Mark had no choice, yet he never considered complaining. On the factory floor, there was no air conditioning and no special treatment for the boss's son. "I've got a lot to prove," he thought, "because my dad gave me the job." His internal standards began to click into gear. It was clear that given the mandate to work, children like Mark were quite happy to do so even when they had little financial motivation or need.

In the case of Jeremy, his father had been raised in great wealth inherited from both sides of his family. On his mother's side, they could trace their affluence back to before the Civil War; on his father's side, the fortune was made in the early days of Wall Street. Yet the message Jeremy's father conveyed to his son and two daughters was: "Put your own mark on the world—I don't want you walking around entitled. You are what *you* are; don't expect things to be given to you." Though their family history was illustrious, Jeremy's father focused more on the present day, emphasizing strength of character and virtue over birthright or experience. He fully expected his children to stand on their own two feet and make a name for themselves. This is an especially powerful message given that the father himself was an inheritor. Instead of taking the obvious route of a life of ease, he chose instead to focus on achievement and meritocracy, saying, "Earn your way; don't ever expect someone else to do it for you."

As young children, David and his siblings knew they were eventually expected to get jobs and earn money. "It was like a mandate of the family," said David. "When you turn 16, you have to get a summer job." As a consequence, one after another they went out and found work. So it was not only a given that they would do as their older sibling had done, but the prospect was also far less intimidating, as they had already seen the process in action. They did not question or resist the mandate, but took it as par for the course and embraced it with equanimity.

The stories that Henry's parents emphasized were similar. Growing up outside New York, he was part of an affluent community yet always understood that it was his responsibility to earn his own way in life. Both his parents worked hard, the extended family worked hard, and the kids were expected to work hard, too. "You go to work and you take care of your own life, and you don't go beyond those limits" is the message he took with him into adult life.

What Young Adults Learn from Work

There are chores, there's homework, and there are jobs that children do for family and friends. But what does it mean to have a "real" job? Does the legitimacy of the job relate to the nature of the work itself, payment for effort, or something less easily defined? From our perspective, young adults experience the world of "real" work in a variety of ways, but most meaningfully when the parents' influence on the working person is minimized. As much as possible, the young person should feel they obtained the job and succeeded, or didn't succeed, on their own merits—not on the back of their parents' influence or affluence. Real work involves interaction with the outside world when you are held accountable on the basis of *how you perform* rather than who you are or where you come from.

Early work teaches affluent children several formative lessons that would be difficult, if not impossible, for them to learn elsewhere: They learn to earn money and be resourceful; they get much-needed social exposure; they understand how to be a subordinate and to work hard. In addition, it gives them a taste for the deeper payoffs that one derives from the experience of work. Experimental psychologist Martin Seligman, who outlined the twenty-four character traits he believes contribute to making people happy and successful, wrote in his latest book, *Flourish,* that these key factors help individuals thrive:

- positive emotion

- engagement with what one is doing

- good relationships

- a sense of meaning and accomplishment[33]

Work contributes significantly to our chances of experiencing each of these. Without the opportunity to engage with the outside world in a meaningful way, we deprive ourselves of the opportunity to learn about others and ourselves. Seligman also emphasizes that people of any age can be taught focus, delayed gratification, and grit—all of which are important to developing a sense of potential and purpose.

As Kent from California explained, he learned from his father that "money isn't the most important thing in the world.

It's the value of work that's important—doing something meaningful." By working odd jobs as a teenager and then a variety of real jobs once he entered college, he learned that "work has an inherent value because it's contributing something to society, and you're not just being a sponge."

Making the concept of money more tangible

One of the most powerful lessons young adults learn from working is how to earn money, and how to regulate spending the money they earned. It is an unfortunate reality that many wealthy children miss this foundational step. You need to learn how to earn money before learning how to spend it, invest it, and give it away. Because many wealthy children never experience this first step, they struggle with a lack of ownership over their money and really understanding the value of a dollar. This can set them up for psychological struggles as well as various concrete problems managing their expenses.

Eve and her siblings, from the San Francisco area, each opened bank accounts when they got their first jobs as teenagers. Any money they earned went straight into their accounts, and when they wanted to spend money during the school year they knew where to find it. As a result, when Eve wanted to go to the movies she never had to ask for money. "Because I had my own money," she said, "I had a better understanding of how much things cost and how to be on my own."

"I knew I shouldn't spend more than I had," she explained. "That was a definite lesson I learned along the way. It taught me not to spend all my money at once." She understood the most basic equation: You earn money, you put it in the bank, you take out what you need.

Her brother, David, vividly recounted the thrill of managing his own funds. "I still remember opening my first bank account and depositing my money," David said. "I had a passbook and they'd print the deposit amount on it and then the new balance—it was exciting. It felt like, this is great having my own money." Is there another experience quite as simple and straightforward as this one? Allowing children to see the fruits of their own labors multiply over time by dint of their own effort and persistence is a tangible gift, the effects of which are felt for years to come.

The sense of ownership over money that was gained by earning it through paid work proved to be so galvanizing for our inheritors that we heard about it over and over again. Getting a real job outside the home is one of the most critical steps a young person takes toward establishing a sense of personal responsibility.

They develop autonomy and resourcefulness

It's well known that in current workplace culture, people job hop constantly. According to the Bureau of Labor Statistics,[34] the average person born between 1957 and 1964 held over 11 jobs between the ages of 18 and 46 (and nearly half those jobs were held between the ages of 18 and 24). Another recent survey[35] shows that for younger adults the statistics are even more extreme: about 90 percent of Millennials (those born between 1977 and 1997) expect to stay in a job less than three years, meaning 15 to 20 job changes in one career. Today's reality is that young people need to be equipped to handle all aspects of job searching on their own—from figuring out what they want to do and what they are actually capable of doing, to landing interviews, getting job offers, and finally, maintaining their careers over time.

Jane's parents expected their children to be resourceful when it came to finding work. While they were willing to drive Jane and her brother around and make sure they had the right attire for their workplaces, the children themselves had to piece the rest of the puzzle together. Stephen remembers creating his first résumé on his mother's computer and sending it out to local electronics stores while looking for a job debugging computers. When she was 12, his sister Jane scoured the local paper looking for listings for babysitting jobs. While intimidating, after job hunting once or twice they began to feel more comfortable putting themselves out there. It toughened them up to face inevitable rejections, and gave them confidence when they landed a spot doing something they were excited about.

Many kids started small-scale entrepreneurial ventures that gave them a sense of their power and potential. Take one of the interviewees, Matthew. In his early teens, Matthew suffered from depression, often feeling especially guilty because he was aware of the privileges he enjoyed coming from a family of means yet he felt inexplicably despondent. Growing up in Washington, D.C., with parents who emphasized philanthropy, Matthew often felt lost and angry, and he would try to excise these feelings by shopping. After working with the local chapter of his Boys & Girls club, he discovered a talent for making videos. From that moment on everything changed.

At age 15, Matthew traveled to Laos with his father and made a promotional video for a charity organization there. He charged less than a professional would, but received a significant fee for a teenager. The sense of accomplishment he felt from creating something that was so highly valued was incredible. "When I really started achieving on my own, I became a much happier person," he said. "The majority of it was finding my own identity . . . I've always woken up knowing what I need to do that day in order to achieve the next step."

For Matthew, the first step was believing in his own abilities, and knowing that his efforts were both constructive and valued. After finishing high school, he took some time off and then finished college in just two and a half years. "I always knew I could make money if I needed to," he explained. "I understood a lot better the value of a dollar. I understood how you can leverage opportunity and leverage wealth and I had a much healthier way to feel good."

Matthew understood viscerally that even though he might struggle with health issues, he had skills that could be put to good use. This was powerful knowledge that continues to fuel his confidence to this day.

Bursting the bubble of privilege

Many well-off modern families encourage their kids to engage in volunteer work so they can see firsthand the reality of how less wealthy people live and struggle. While they do this for good reasons and to good effect, the experience of stepping in and offering charity is very different than stepping into a situation and offering your skills as an equal or a subordinate.

When young people work with others from different walks

of life, they see themselves as part of a greater picture; they are participating in a story bigger than they are and, maybe for the first time in their lives, they have an awareness and appreciation of the realities of life beyond what they have known. Though David's parents had made a fortune in the packaged food business, that didn't stop them from expecting him to go out into the world and earn his spending money. His first ever job was as a dishwasher at a dockside grill in his small town just north of San Francisco. "I actually had a lot of fun working in the kitchen. It taught me about working on a team, whether they were a lot older or my age," he says, "and about learning to influence people." That's a powerful lesson to learn as the youngest employee among a team of more experienced workers.

With some wonder in his voice, David recalled the variety of characters he was exposed to in that job. "A lot of people working as short-order cooks were on leave from prison, for smaller crimes like drugs or DUI. I learned that these people deserve a second chance. I didn't have to be their best friend," he said, "but I could maybe learn something from them."

This variety of experience contributes to the development of social intelligence, which helps people navigate complex social environments and relationships. Additionally, giving wealthy children opportunities to step outside their comfort zone leads to a renewed perspective on their own lives, and the role their family wealth does or does not play for them. Eve, who started working as a babysitter when she was 13 earning $3 an hour, went on to take a variety of jobs at the local mall where she made minimum wage. One year she worked at Kay Bee Toys. Then she worked at Abercrombie. For a couple of months, she worked as a salesperson at Bloomingdale's. Meeting people who made a living at this wage level was a real eye-opener and later in life gave her an appreciation for jobs that paid more.

Daniel was a busboy in a restaurant in an industrial section of Boston for almost two years; there he saw a "whole other walk of life; one of the women who was a waitress had been a prostitute." This threw into relief the advantages he had growing up and led him to work harder to prove himself worthy of his circumstances. When Taylor worked as a receptionist in a hotel for one summer, she learned that "no one really owes you anything." Ever since then, she felt that parents who give their children *anything at all* are being incredibly generous.

To be a good leader you have to be a good follower

Growing up, Bill spent many hours at his father's side in the family-run department store in Illinois. A gregarious boy with a tendency to be curious and comfortable around adults, he would accompany his father to work on weekend mornings and keep himself busy among the aisles and in the back offices. Sometimes he did small tasks for his father like sharpening pencils, and other times he helped employees fold shirts or sweep floors. "I'd bother everybody," he said, "and go through the cash drawers looking for buffalo-head nickels and silver coins." It was during that time observing life in the store that he developed a sense of the value of work and the satisfaction of setting and achieving goals.

Early on, Bill knew he wanted to become a businessman. After graduating from college, he worked for his father briefly before being accepted into a prestigious training program where he was paid to learn and work. He felt lucky to be accepted, and pride in having achieved it on his own. "I was a low man on the totem pole, but I would have done it for free," he said. All the jobs he'd done stacking shelves and working the register taught him about the value every individual brings to a business, whether it's the CEO or the sales clerk. "The most effective leaders today are the ones who are out there in front, dealing face to face with their teams," he said. "It's about treating people as equal from a dignity perspective, because they are."

Learning to be a subordinate can be hard, but as the saying goes: *To be a good leader, first you have to be a good follower.* For wealthy kids, when an adult other than a parent is judging them and telling them what to do, they learn rather quickly to take responsibility for their attitudes and actions. These adult children learn to think from another person's perspective, and understand that everyone can and should be bringing something to the table. They become aware of their own role as part of the larger picture, and their own responsibilities. And, perhaps most importantly for affluent children, they learn about self-control.

Kent, who began working in jobs outside the home well before college, joined the Navy when he graduated, where the qualities of leadership were further honed through enforced subordination. Now in his daily life as CEO of a burgeoning software company, he traces his attention to detail and his ability to lead a group of diverse employees to his experiences learning to follow.

They gain confidence in their abilities

Children these days are accustomed to copious praise from parents—some argue it has become too much of a good thing. But when young people in a work environment are assessed on the value of their efforts by an objective observer, they are learning something valuable about themselves. Sometimes, after years of being "nagged" by parents and treated like a child, they're surprised and empowered to find that they are considered by other adults to be capable and mature. This contributes to a sense of optimism and zest that are part of being a well-rounded, happy, and productive adult.

When David began his work at the dockside restaurant as a dishwasher, he was simply seeking to earn some spending money. But within two months he was promoted, first to driving patrons in a van from the parking lot to the restaurant and then to being a host in the dining room. He learned the direct correlation between hard work and success.

Kent, who worked in the art supply shop when he was 15 years old, soon realized that he was more competent than the 50-year-old manager. Quite aside from learning self-management skills such as getting to work on time, he began to develop a sense of his leadership abilities. Jack began working on film sets while still in high school, and between junior and senior year of college he was a production assistant on a small but well-received independent film. "I felt that I was more capable than a lot of the people I was working for," he recalled. "I was spoken to as someone who had a lot of potential. They said, *'When you get out of college, look me up! When you do your first film, call me!'*" The vote of confidence this remark gave him fueled his drive to persevere through years of struggle in the creative field until he could achieve critical as well as financial success from his work.

Blood, sweat, and tears

How do young people develop the traits of grit and self-control that are so critical to finding success in the work world and happiness in life? How do they learn about time management, goal setting, and resilience? Turns out, the answer is simple: by getting and keeping a job.

While David remembers his stint in the restaurant quite fondly, especially the interesting people he worked with, he also recalls putting in endless hours and feeling stressed by the variety of responsibilities he had. He had to drive to get to work and make sure to leave enough time to negotiate traffic so he'd arrive punctually. He put in at least ten hours a week on top of his school days; managing that as well as his homework taught him about effectively managing his time.

The summer between 11th and 12th grades, William, who grew up in Manhattan as the son of a food importer, was sent to France to work in a wine factory for a month. "I knew the people I was working with were charged with teaching me to work hard," said William, but he didn't realize until he got there what hard work really meant. "I had to bust my ass, and I'll never forget it." For him, learning about expectation and effort was invaluable, and helped him put his own experiences and outlook into perspective: "It made me appreciate that there are people who work on assembly lines and it's really, really tough."

Gaby admits to being "kind of lazy" by nature. Unmarried

and without children, she likes to sleep late and meet friends for brunch on weekends in Philadelphia. One of her first real jobs was working for a high-end auction house on their catalogues. It turned out to be an astonishingly time-consuming and stressful job.

"I didn't have any concept of hard work at the time," she says. Frequently, her home phone would ring at 7:00 in the morning and it would be her boss, calling her to talk about work. Her boss recognized that because of her upbringing, she hadn't learned to work hard. He took her under his wing and held her to demanding standards. While at the time she thought, *'I don't need this, I'm a rich kid,'* she now recognizes the critical lessons he was teaching her. "It took years for me to get it. But my boss knew what he was doing."

She also discovered that she loved going to work because she was part of a group with specific goals every day. The work setting provided her the structure she was having trouble setting for herself. She learned about delayed gratification and developing habits that made her grow to love the routine of work.

Money Isn't Everything

Wealthy parents aren't alone. For eons, aristocracy has dealt with this problem of how to teach the younger generation to be productive and fuel their desire to work. The British royal family have navigated this path surprisingly well in many cases. "We were very fortunate in where we grew up and what we had when we were growing up," said Peter Phillips, Queen Elizabeth II's grandson, "but one thing that was always made very, very clear to both of us by our parents was, 'This is not an easy life. You will have to go out and earn your living.' So we always had a strong work ethic instilled in us from a very early age."[36]

Parents have a responsibility to help their children learn about the value of hard work by insisting they get real jobs. Too much pampering and hand-holding only inhibits affluent children from feeling the intense satisfaction of forging ahead under their own terms with lives they design and pay for through their own imagination and effort.

Getting and retaining a job is not only about earning a living—it's about finding a purposeful way to spend a lifetime. The vast majority of individuals who do not have satisfying work toward which to apply themselves day to day quickly become lost and bored. Work provides an avenue for self-fulfillment and joy that few other activities can offer.

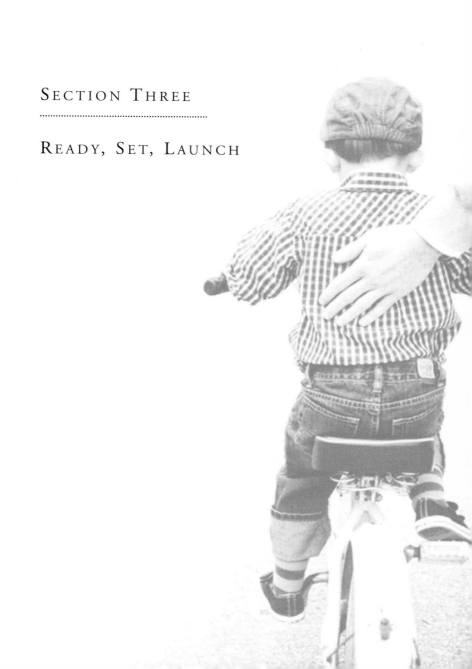

SECTION THREE

READY, SET, LAUNCH

....

CHAPTER FIVE

After College, You're on Your Own

The 20's are a transitional time when young adults straddle two worlds, relying on their parents and mentors for guidance and support while progressively building toward their own, independent view of the world. This growing self-sufficiency provides the framework upon which they build satisfying autonomous lives. At this critical juncture, parents are charged with the difficult task of finding the balance between supporting them and letting them go.

After college comes a vital period in a young person's development during which the lessons they've learned throughout childhood are put into play. Handled well, these youngsters are set up for a healthy start to adult life; handled poorly, and there is a strong possibility that they will continue to struggle with these issues for much of their adult lives.

We heard from our interviewees that it was during their 20's that many of the markers of success were established and solidified. Typically this is when young adults begin to

- form their own separate adult identities and make decisions accordingly;

- develop autonomy around money, both on an abstract and a practical level;

- define success for themselves and establish their vocational goals;

- learn through experience that they have the resilience and wherewithal to navigate adult life.

In an ironic twist, much of the advice given to parents by the wealth management industry at this point in a young person's life is at direct cross-purposes with this reality. For example, tax experts often advise parents to make use of the gift tax exemption to give their children annual gifts (currently up to $28,000 if both parents give). Yet when parents make these gifts to their children, the money often ends up in their child's bank account, easily accessible and with no guidance on what it is to be used for. An unwelcome surprise to parents is that young adults can often live off this level of limited funding, which then ends up delaying the process of living independently.

Additionally, this period of a child's life frequently comes at a time when parents have reached their 50's and 60's and are beginning to think about their own legacy. They want to see their money at play in their children's lives, whether by helping them buy their first home, funding a certain lifestyle, or investing in a new business.

But as we will see, it is precisely during this critical developmental period that parents and children are better served by taking a long-term view, and choosing to foster separation and independence over other concerns. While the instinct to give children a leg up through continued financial support is understandable, acting upon this instinct can be profoundly destabilizing over time. All too often we see young adults who fail to launch successfully because their parents remain too enmeshed in their daily lives, depriving them of the opportunity to mature right at the precise moment in their development when it is so critical.

Challenges help you grow

In the 1950s, a German-born psychologist named Erik Erikson established a theory of psychosocial development that emphasized the environment in which children are raised rather than focusing on the primacy of the id, an instinctive and inherited force. This is of particular interest to professionals working with inheritors because growing up with money heavily impacts the home environment—and not always in beneficial ways.

Erikson believed that in order to develop a healthy personality, a young person must learn to deal with and overcome five basic challenges that correlate with specific developmental milestones. These challenges are: building an attitude of basic trust, developing autonomy, using initiative, being industrious, and having a clear sense of personal identity. He believed that when these challenges are met and survived, the child has a greater chance of being psychologically intact.

If appropriate intellectual and emotional development comes from making an effort to overcome life's tribulations, then it stands to reason that when those challenges are circumvented or dealt with poorly, there is far greater chance of later struggles. In his book, *How Children Succeed,* Paul Tough quotes the head-master of an elite New York prep school lamenting the lack of resilience in his students: "Our kids don't put up with a lot of suffering. They don't have a threshold for it," he says. "We try to talk to parents about having to sort of make it OK for there to be challenge, because that's where the learning happens."[37]

Frequently, wealth enables children to avoid important challenges—minimizing pain or discomfort in the short term, while increasing reliance on family funds in the long term. Foot-ball coach Vince Lombardi famously said, "It's easy to have faith in yourself and have discipline when you're a winner . . . what you've got to have is faith and discipline when you're not yet a winner." A golden life of winning streaks cannot be guaranteed.

Author John L. Levy points out some of the fallout that arises when the wealthy avoid these regular challenges: "The crises and challenges that Erikson postulates as necessary for healthy development of the personality can be avoided, diminished or delayed by the person who is protected by the comfort and secu-rity that money provides."[38]

For instance, wealthy kids often feel alienated from "regu-lar" folks and can be distrustful as a consequence. Autonomy becomes hard to establish if inheritors do not value or take pride in their accomplishments, and attribute them to money and posi-tion rather than to ability. Feeling inadequate and dependent on others can lead to guilt (we heard a lot about this, even from our successful inheritors). Fear of failure and lack of purpose in turn diminish initiative and industry. Parents' own successes combined with their continued interference often overshadow their children's hopes and dreams, and can foster and even exacerbate this insecurity.

And yet in our interviews we heard stories of struggle and triumph that suggest inheritors are by no means destined to immaturity and dissatisfaction because of their experiences growing up in affluence. Over and over again, we heard a strong undercurrent of pride when young people felt ownership of the money they were spending, when they were able to call the shots in their own lives, and when they felt free of meddling parental oversight. They learned from their mistakes and enjoyed their independence. These inheritors were able to form appropriate expectations about how to live independently driven adult lives. They enjoyed the feeling of self-directed striving toward individual pursuits and the satisfaction of hard-earned successes.

But in order for their children to pass these valuable and necessary milestones, parents had to be willing to let them strike out on their own first.

Self-determination leads to success

Jane is now recently engaged and living and working in New York. As a teenager in South Carolina, her parents emphasized academics, but also encouraged her independence by allowing her to try different activities and part-time jobs that she felt drawn to. A highly social person, Jane worked selling beauty supplies at a hair salon for a while and then spent a number of years waitressing during college. After graduation, she had no doubts that she could take care of herself. "There was always the expectation that after college they [the parents] were done," she explains. "I was smart enough to know that I needed to have some kind of path so I could get a job and live on my own." By the time she graduated college, she already had a strong sense of her independence and capabilities.

Remember self-determination theory from the last chapter? "When self-determined," authors Deci and Ryan write, "people experience a sense of freedom to do what is interesting, personally important and vitalizing."[39] Deci and Ryan argue that in order to feel self-determined and to experience the kind of volitional engagement that makes people happy, individuals need to experience autonomy, competence, and relatedness. This was borne out in the stories we heard from our interviewees. There was a deep sense of satisfaction from accomplishing something on their own (being autonomous and competent) that was missing if they felt others were somehow responsible for their success.

Pride in doing it on their own

The actor Armie Hammer's family fortune came from oil. "We like sort of living hand to mouth," he said in a recent interview in which he explained that he and his wife do not live off a trust fund. "It makes you appreciate the time when you don't have to live like that. We don't want to go to my parents and tuck our tails between our legs and be like, 'Can you help us?' We wanted to be our own adults."[40] This is a mantra we heard repeated in various ways throughout hours of interviews: Inheritors felt most successful when they did not rely on their parents for support after moving out of the family home.

Most of us remember saving up for that item our parents

thought too frivolous when we were kids. The joy of being able to buy it with our own saved-up pennies made the choice to invest all the more personal and meaningful. If the money was wasted, we learned a lesson about the difference between want and need, quality and quantity, fads and longevity. If the item proved worthwhile, our satisfaction was all the greater for having spent our own money. And we can all remember the first big purchase we made on our own as young adults, whether it was a car, a down payment on a home, or our first major trip with friends. It was the same with our interviewees.

Bill and his siblings grew up on the outskirts of Chicago, where his family's department store chain was headquartered. Between carpooling, getting rides from friends, borrowing cars (once they got their permits), and being ferried back and forth by their parents, Bill and his siblings managed to get around pretty well. In the summer of 1978 when Bill went to college, he decided he wanted a car of his own and bought himself a used Dodge Dart for $40. "Dad had allowed me to use his hand-me-down cars before," he said, "but I didn't have the sense of self-worth and gratification that I did with that $40 investment in that car!"

His voice warmed while recounting his story; the car was only a secondhand rusted-out junker, but he had loved it. In fact, Bill enjoyed his $40 car more than he would have enjoyed being given a $40,000 Corvette. "When you support yourself instead of stuff being given to you, it means more than anything," he said. Another interviewee talked about buying her first car, an old Audi, with money she saved up over three years, and echoed Bill's sentiment: "The first thing you appreciate is the thing you buy on your own," she said.

On the other hand, when parents give children things they could save up for and buy on their own—whether trinkets when they're little or a car once they're older—they are depriving them of the genuine and lasting satisfaction of *doing it on their own*. Children of wealth often wrestle with the sense that they do not deserve the perks they are privileged to enjoy, whether it's summering in the Alps, driving a Range Rover, or snagging a coveted first job. They live with a constant sense of inadequacy as they question whether they really deserve the bounty they are receiving. Then, in a defensive move to thwart the possible risk of failure, they may be quick to underplay their efforts, or underestimate their own abilities. But when affluent children save for a sought-after purchase, the sweetness of achievement is doubly enjoyed because it came from their own labors.

Handing over the reins

As a teenager, Kent worked part time in an art supply store and was given total control over how he spent the money he made. "If I wanted something, I'd have to save up for it. On the flip side, I could buy what I wanted if I was paying with my own money," he said.

While his parents continued to support him throughout college, including paying his tuition, it was understood that Kent was expected to go it on his own once he graduated. "I was financially independent from age 21 on," he said. "On a psychological level, that meant controlling my own destiny."

Feeling beholden to parents can be a burden for a young person starting out in life. While every parent wants to be appreciated and respected for the help they offer, few want their adult children to feel bound or inhibited by that help. What feels to a parent like a gift can be a weight holding a child back from maturing fully. Instead of dealing with the natural challenges brought on by becoming an adult that Erikson outlined, too many affluent children skip those bumps in the road, failing to learn how to take full responsibility for their decisions and actions. When you're not calling the shots it's all too easy to become a passive player in your own life.

In Kent's case, his father's strong personality risked hindering the development of his son's internal motivation. Instead, because he encouraged Kent to become independent early on, his son was afforded a sense of psychological freedom that otherwise would have been elusive. And with that freedom came the burden of responsibility: Kent learned to plan, assess, avoid or accept risk, and then live with the consequences. He developed a sense of purpose and drive that was a direct result of his parents giving him the reins and allowing him to become more self-sufficient. As he explained, "If you [parents] try to control everything, you overuse your authority."

There is immense pride in ownership. It's often said that *he who owns the gold makes the rules.* Kent said that asking for money so wounded his sense of pride that he avoided it at all costs. "My father, for better or for worse, frequently reminded me that he was calling the shots," he explained. "I didn't like being in that position." Kids not only feel the desire to be in charge of their own lives, but they also want to prove to their parents and themselves that they are capable of handling this responsibility.

Similarly, Bill, who bought himself the used Dodge Dart, discovered as a young man heading into the "real" world that he was motivated to work hard, make his own choices, and live with his mistakes. After college, he was expected to take care of himself; it came as no surprise and he fully expected to be able to handle it. "I never resented that there were trust funds set up for me; but I always wanted to not live off that trust and make it on my own," he said.

When Sam was a child, her mother no longer worked outside the home, but she'd had a thriving career in sales before stopping work to raise her three children. Sam's father works in a high-profile financial position based in Houston. Since early childhood, Sam has been aware of how the family is viewed by the community, and this drives her to want to establish her own place in the world. "In college, I did feel this sense that I should be making my own money and that making my own money and living off it somehow meant I was a distinct person, *my own person* in a way," she said. "I never want people to think I didn't make it on my own—even my family members. There's this rich-kid, do-nothing stereotype and I want to do the opposite of that."

This of course begs the question: What steps can and should parents take to encourage their children to become financially independent? Rather than giving kids everything, how can parents help them earn things for themselves? These are important questions that we tackle in the next chapter.

Consequences of not feeling real "ownership"

When William was 13, his father sold his business and his family experienced a stark transition from living a "normal" life to a life of great wealth, relocating from their village walk-up to a Park Avenue duplex. Once William was off at college, there was an ad hoc relationship regarding transfers of money from his parents that was confusing. "If I wanted to do something I'd ask my father and he'd send me a check," William said. "Sometimes he'd send the check late and I'd have to call him and ask for it. There was all sorts of conflict. In grad school and then afterwards, I thought about doing different things but I realized I needed to earn money so I wouldn't be beholden to Dad."

One of the ongoing problems this uneasy dynamic around money created for William was a continuing sense that the family money was never truly his own, even once he was a fully independent adult making excellent money as a consultant. When thinking about his personal failures and successes, for example, he counts the demise of his first marriage as a failure inextricably linked to this question of *whose money is it anyway?*

"My ex-wife saw all this money out there that I never really felt was mine," William explained. "She felt she had to play this role, going to charity events and being on boards—and I had to pay for it all with money I didn't feel was my own."

It wasn't until later in his career, when his own earnings outstripped the money that he'd inherited, that his conflicted relationship with his father began to improve. "When I wasn't fully paying for my own life . . . it felt like I was being infantilized by my father," he said.

Earning the money they spend—*"doing it on my own"*—is what helps inheritors establish a healthy sense of self and emotional independence. Without this, they can struggle for years with figuring out how to feel truly worthy. Sarah is the graphic designer from New Orleans, striking out on her own in Seattle. She lives in an attractive but modest one-bedroom apartment downtown with views of Puget Sound. Once she decided it was time to live alone rather than with roommates, her parents helped her create a budget so she could figure out what she could afford. "But there was lack of clarity on what the [trust] money was for," she said. "I wasn't sure if rent was the right thing to use the money for. It still felt like *their* money."

She had a sense that her job should be able to cover her rent because her trust fund money was not supposed to be spent on those sorts of expenditures—that money should be tapped for larger, more important needs. She hated the fact that she had to rely on her parents to help her with the rent. It was only once she began earning more money and was able to contribute more and more to her daily living expenses that she felt truly "grown up."

Another interviewee expressed similar feelings. "I think there's a kind of discomfort with spending money that isn't mine," said John, now an art gallery owner in his late 30's. Like William's former wife, John's spouse has also been perplexed about her husband's conflicted and complicated relationship with money. "My wife doesn't understand my angst about it," he said.

Freedom from a parent's legacy

A parent or grandparent's immense financial success can lead to inheritors suffering feelings of diminishment, guilt, and lack of motivation. Sometimes the next generation does not feel it can live up to a parent's successes. But being given the freedom to explore in their 20's, on their own terms using their own efforts to fund their explorations, appears to be a critical element in inheritors' establishing a sound sense of self-worth. Even William and John, who struggled through some rough patches, have come out in the end having made peace with their inheritances. They have both found ways to be successful on their own terms.

"Successful personal development seems to demand a personal journey where the individual separates from the family, and does something real, visible and important on his or her own," write family enterprise experts Fredda Herz Brown, Ph.D. and Dennis Jaffe, Ph.D. "This is a time of opportunity; there is a window available to educate our young people about the transience of money and the need to develop an ability to rely on one's self."[41] Our interviewees echoed this theme: Given the opportunity to launch, they took it, and the pride they felt stayed with them and fueled much of their later success.

It is striking that William, who inherited his wealth and is now raising children who will in turn inherit, said that he wants them "ultimately to live off of the money they earn, not inherited wealth." While William talked glowingly about his experiences growing up, an undercurrent of discomfort ran through our conversation. We were into the second hour when we began talking about the lessons he wanted to impart to his daughter. He took a moment to think about the question.

"I want her to be really *free*," he started. This comes from the fact that he had to deal with the psychological costs of not feeling entirely free and independent from his family. This colors how he sees himself; even now he struggles with defining himself as a "successful" inheritor despite enjoying a happy family life and a career that he loves and that pays well.

The surprising case for . . . independent travel

After about our tenth interview, we began noticing a distinct pattern in the stories we were hearing. Many of our successful inheritors talked at great length—and with discernable nostalgia—about breaking free of their lifestyles and heading out to explore the larger world after college. It turns out that an extended, self-financed adventure during which wealthy young people live life "like the locals" was often life changing for them.

Encouraging young adults to cut the cord and navigate hurdles on their own gives them a chance to engage in the maturing process outlined by Erik Erikson. It's an opportunity for wealthy children who may otherwise have been stymied in these developmental stages to actually experience and manage them on their own. They throw off the mantle of their parents' successes and identities, and discover the inner reserves they may not previously have realized they had. They learn to support themselves, managing the logistics of an itinerant lifestyle without help or interference; form an identity separate from the family; explore the work world on their own terms; and get outside the bubble of their upbringing.

Jack, who spent a couple of months working on an isolated island when he was just 16, grew up in the old orange groves of Arizona in a spacious house staffed by two full-time staff. He attended private school and spent the summers in one of his family's two country houses—one in the mountains outside Phoenix and the other in Nantucket. Upon graduation, he decided to return to Berlin, where he had spent a semester abroad a few years earlier. "For whatever reason, I told myself I wanted to do it without spending any of the money I'd been given," he told us. "It was the one moment in my life when I spent zero of those dollars."

For a year and a half Jack lived in various run-down apartments in Prenzlauerberg, finding work as a DJ, party promoter, and English teacher. Life was not always easy. There were times when his living conditions were poor and when he didn't have enough money for a decent meal. "But it felt good," he said. "That experience more than anything gave me an appreciation of the privileges of having money."

He developed a strong sense of his capabilities, realizing that he did not need his parents' money to survive because he was resourceful enough to find jobs that would cover his bills. And he learned that not only could he survive in conditions that were less glamorous than those he was accustomed to, but he could actually thrive. Even now he finds himself choosing thrift over profligacy, and takes pride in leaving a small footprint.

When parents allow their children to set off on their own, without interfering to question what they're doing or to help them live a more comfortable lifestyle, they are giving them the gift of recalibrating what "normal" means. Sometimes it's the first time children raised in affluence truly understand how other people live.

Speeding up, not delaying, maturation

Many parents are leery of gap years or taking extended time off during or after college for freeform travel. They see it as an excuse to postpone the work of "real life;" an opportunity to indulge in a carefree existence that delays maturation. The irony is that we found the opposite to be true—provided the inheritors plan and execute the travel *using their own means.*

It's true that when a trip is merely a delaying tactic, or an excuse for some fun, it is less worthwhile. Gaby asked her parents to support her in taking a six-month trip through Asia. Her parents saw it as a boondoggle and told her she either needed to find work instead, or pay for the trip herself. Since she hadn't planned on paying her own way, she decided to forgo the trip and signed up for an internship at a small book printer in Pittsburgh instead. This opened the door to working in publishing; before long she found her vocation. In her case, traveling on her parents' dime would not have afforded her the valuable lessons her internship did.

Yet for many young adults, taking time off and orchestrating an experience that takes them out of their comfort zone can be an ideal way to discover what they're really made of. It can prove to themselves—and others—that they are more than the sum of their background and their prior experiences.

Earlier, we wrote about Henry, who grew up in the suburbs of New York attending parties at the Yacht Club and perfecting his golf game. A promising student, he was accepted at Yale where he proceeded to spend a lot of time chasing fun and only a little time studying. Since he wasn't flourishing, he proposed to his parents that he take a year off to work and travel. When discussing how to pay for the trip, his parents agreed the money should come from Henry's own funds. "The only idea I had was that I wanted to go as far away as I could from my background, so I picked Australia. I had this romantic idea of striking out," he said.

And strike out he did. When he landed in Australia, he

bought a car for $400 which he used to drive 10,000 miles throughout the continent. For six months he worked in a cattle ranch, whose serpentine driveway was over 40 miles long. Working with men who had never even seen the ocean, and had most certainly never heard of Yale, Henry discovered that what mattered more than who he was and where he came from was what he was made of. "It stripped away all the forms of identity I thought I was built on. I began to understand the force of personality," he said. "It's the impression you're making on people that's important, not where you came from."

Most critically, Henry's self-perception was indelibly altered. "The way I saw myself changed. The context of who I am makes no sense at all there—it's about things like, how well do you handle yourself? Can you do this job? How enjoyable are you to be with?"

At the end of his trip, Henry circumnavigated the Pacific Islands on a trawler hauling fish. "It was very humbling and that was a great thing. I got more out of it than I expected to," he said. He also learned about sweat equity. "These guys worked extremely hard. It never occurred to me that I wouldn't hold up my end of the bargain. I was watching people and thinking, *It's incumbent on me to do that too.*'"

During his year of adventure, Henry grew up more quickly than he would have by going through the motions in college. By the time he returned to school, he was a changed man. He had escaped the milieu where his name, ancestry, privilege, and education were known and in so doing was able to define for himself who he was at his core. It was freeing to be recognized on his own terms and to understand how to treat people so that he, in turn, was respected and liked, regardless of his privilege.

He discovered in himself a capacity to endure and flourish that he'd never before had the chance to test. Interestingly, in Henry's case, his experiences on this trip actually led to his pursuing a fulfilling and economically fruitful career in the travel field. He started as a travel writer and documentarian and is now a producer of content for cable and broadcast television.

Matteo, who was born to wealth in northern India and moved to the United States at age 18, learned about self-sufficiency and hard work through leaving home. After overhearing people who did not know him referring to his family's money as a reason for his successes, he decided he needed to break free from his family's shadow. "They weren't giving me credit that I was working really hard, but were attributing it to the fact that I was born into the right family," he said. "If I stayed, I would always be someone's son, not myself."

Moving away and setting up a life for himself was not always easy. There were years in college when he survived on only one meal a day, but he was driven to make a name for himself. Going to a place where all that counted was the intensity and quality of his efforts rather than who is family was turned out to be the key that unlocked the future and allowed him to be truly comfortable in his own skin for the first time.

A true gift

Clearly, autonomy produces a deep sense of pride. Our interviews highlighted the fact that nothing truly rivals the satisfaction young people feel when they can support their lifestyles and when they have earned their purchases through their own effort and persistence. Supporting yourself rightfully confers a feeling of self-respect and ownership that affluent children deserve to experience, and yet in their efforts to help, parents sometimes actually rob their children of this critical experience. This problem seems to be more about the parents than the children. The parents' compulsion to "help"—usually in order to manage their feelings of discomfort or guilt when a child's living circumstances are sub par—in fact does the very opposite.

In contrast, what we see in our successful inheritors is that by *not helping* parents are actually giving their child a gift. When a young man named Julian came into money in his mid-20's, he began a correspondence with his trustee via email. The trustee's words to Julian spoke volumes about the self-worth that comes from self-confidence and independence: "As you know, you have been given a great gift from your parents—that is the head on your shoulders, your education, your humility, and your strong values, among many other blessings. The trust is a resource that you have to assist you to fulfill your goals and ambitions and to provide you with a level of financial security. It will never replace the satisfaction you will get from your own successes that I am sure you will have in life." Parents and trustees who emphasize this message do a great service to their kids.

Yet it takes some backbone to support children in separating financially and emotionally when parental instinct is to do just the opposite. This is compounded by a wealth management industry that often centers the conversation on wealth transfer, heightening the parents' natural emotional pull to share the wealth. There is certainly a time and a place for opening the veil and sharing financial details and intentions regarding inheritance, but the right time to do so is not during the inheritors'

20's when they are doing all they can to separate emotionally and financially.

When you feel the impulse to step in and help your children out, always ask yourself: *Help them do what?* The answer should be to help them develop the success traits we saw in our interviewees, outlined in chapter 1. And the reality is that a certain amount of separation and autonomy from parents and their money is a prerequisite for any child to develop these traits. Therefore, at every juncture, ask yourself whether your help—or interference—at this stage in their lives encourages the development of those critical traits, or hinders them. If the honest answer is that your continued financial input will hinder them in the long run, then don't do it. It's unfair and counterproductive to deny your children the pride in succeeding on their own that you yourself experienced.

Perhaps you remember *The Cosby Show* episode when the family is discussing money? One of Bill Cosby's kids says, "None of this would have happened if we weren't so rich," and in response Cosby quips, "Let me get something straight, okay? Your mother and I are rich. You have *nothing.*" While modern parents might cringe at this line and perceive it as flip or cruel (while laughing), it's worth reflecting on this line in the context of the message we heard from our interviewees about how critical independence was to them and how financial gifts from parents were fraught with complication. While tactless, Cosby's point does one thing that many of our interviewees spoke to wanting desperately: It emphasizes freedom. The child is being reminded of their independence from their parents and of their right to make their own way in the world.

It's not such a bad thing for kids in their 20's to focus more on what they can create for themselves than on what has been given to them. The more independence young adults can forge for themselves after college, the easier it will be for them to manage the work, life, and, yes, inheritance challenges they'll inevitably face in their 30's and 40's and onwards throughout adult life. Instead of conveying the message that the family money is theirs to share, it's better at this early stage to tell them: "The money is here; hopefully you'll never have to use it," as many of our inheritors' parents did.

CHAPTER SIX

Navigating the Gray Areas: Yes, We'll Help, but Here's How

It's all very well to tell parents they should be drawing a line in the sand and insisting that their children become financially independent as young adults. In theory, it's quite sensible and straightforward: In order to be truly happy and successful, when young people reach a certain age they need to develop a sense of autonomy, purpose, and confidence in their own abilities. They must find within themselves the motivation to succeed, and learn to live with the consequences of their own decisions. If they don't achieve this, they won't feel a sense of ownership of their own lives—and it is this sense of ownership that is most galvanizing and healthy for the children of the affluent.

Reality, however, presents parents with all sorts of scenarios that make it challenging to put these theories into practice. In every interview we conducted, we heard of instances when parents stepped in to help out. Whether it was contributing to a security deposit for a rental apartment, subsidizing living expenses during a period of transition, or paying for car insurance after an accident sent rates skyrocketing, there were plenty of cases when a parent intervened financially. In many instances, cutting the cord completely seems both impractical and unnecessary.

In this chapter we look at the gray areas. Is it ever healthy to continually subsidize a young person's lifestyle over many years? When and how do you draw the line in order to do the best for your child in the long run? When is saying no actually more like saying *yes* to a child's happiness? Under what circumstances is financial support helpful and when is it harmful?

There is a way to navigate this minefield with confidence: Everything depends on clarity and limits. When parents give children the freedom to separate while providing guidance by establishing clear expectations, it sets them on a road toward a self-directed future with a set of guardrails so they won't crash and burn. How can parents do this given their everyday realities? In our experience, this can be achieved by emphasizing four messages:

- There's value in hard work.

- You may have to try a number of things before you find what you really love.

- While you are finding what you really love, give every effort, no matter how menial, your best shot—you'll learn from it.

- And last but not least: there are established (and *fixed*) parameters within which we as parents will provide financial support.

The passion problem

It's important to talk about the notion of helping children "find their passion," because it's what derails so many parents before, during, and after their child's launch into adulthood. In recent years, there has been increasing emphasis on encouraging young people to "find their passion" or "follow their passion." The argument is that when we love what we do, we do a much better job. As quality of life has progressed from being considered a luxury to aspire toward to being one of the middle class's primary goals, emphasis has shifted to this notion that work—and by implication, careers—should reflect and build upon an inchoate inner longing, an intuitive sense of rightness. As a result, young adults expect to be magically drawn to a certain field because it is what they are "destined" to do.

Judging by the number of blog posts on this particular topic on its website, the *Harvard Business Review* considers the idea of following your passion particularly misleading and destructive for the latest generation of achievers. "The verb 'follow' implies that you start by identifying a passion and then match this pre-existing calling to a job," writes Cal Newport in a post entitled "Solving Gen Y's Passion Problem." "Because the passion precedes the job, it stands to reason that you should love your work from the very first day."[42] This leads to early disappointment and a lack of grit in sticking things through, which in turn feeds the cycle of never becoming expert enough in a particular field to achieve a feeling of satisfaction.

This modern notion of finding your passion is problematic for the wealthy on numerous fronts. This emphasis is often heightened in affluent families because inheritors can afford to take the time to find just the right vocation. There is a natural tendency to think that family money should allow young adults to engage only in work that they truly love. Why work as a dishwasher earning minimum wage when you could instead be writing the next great American novel or sailing in San Francisco Bay? How do you convince yourself to stick with a job in which you do menial office tasks when you imagined yourself flying around the country making decisions and running meetings?

The idea that passion alights on young adults—that they can bide their time until it miraculously asserts itself—serves only to undermine the development of skills that are integral to fully investing in a vocation. "[The] tough skill-building phase can provide the foundation for a wonderful career," states the HBRpost, "but in this common scenario the 'follow your passion' dogma would tell you that this work is not immediately enjoyable and therefore is not your passion."[43]

The problem is that we've got it backwards. Usually, people find the work they are passionate about only after some long slogs through work that is boring, menial, and/or uncomfortable. Unfortunately, when children are given wealth early, that wealth allows them to walk away before they have done the hard work necessary to find their passion.

In addition, the focus in many affluent families on paying for educational programs can create young adults who become serial students without ever pursuing the job that the education has prepared them for. In this way, even the best-intentioned parents are holding their children back from launching into self-directed lives in which they are able to commit themselves to learning and growing by *doing*, thereby becoming the workers they need to be in order to develop satisfying and meaningful careers.

Another HBR post, called "To Find Happiness, Forget About Passion" by Oliver Segovia, says a whole generation has been subjected to "the grand betrayal of the false idols of passion."[44] So how do wealthy parents help their children avoid spending fruitless years, funded by money they haven't earned themselves, searching for their calling? "We don't find happiness by looking within. We go outside and immerse in the world," writes Segovia. "It's our daily struggles that define us and bring out the best in us, and this lays down the foundation to continuously find fulfillment in what we do even when times get tough."[45]

We saw this very dynamic at play in our successful inheritors. So how did they get it right?

Use objective standards as guidelines

Oftentimes, focusing on talent over passion helps steer parents in the right direction when deciding how much to fund adult children who are not earning their own living. A good determinant of talent is how an outside audience of objective observers receives that child's efforts. If, after a certain amount of time and effort has been invested, your daughter has no audience for her play, or your son's short stories are never published, it may be time to reassess. In these cases, establishing clear boundaries upfront is the key to avoiding painful discussions later when a disappointed child is forced to face reality.

Child psychologist Mel Levine, Ph.D., has written extensively on how to prepare children for a successful adulthood, referring to kids in this in-between stage as "start up adults." In *Ready or Not, Here Life Comes*, he focuses on work readiness, lamenting this generation's lack of preparedness to face the reality of the modern work world. "Having a cause fuels momentum during the start up years, especially when it's combined with some self-discipline and well-honed work habits," he writes. "Unfortunately, some start up adults convince themselves that feeling strongly about a topic or a cause is all it takes to be a leading authority on the subject."[46] Where financial support is concerned, it is important for parents to build an accurate picture for themselves of their children's prospects and potential in their field. Usually, rather than engaging in endless debate about definitions of success, it is more effective to put specific time limits on support.

John began putting on art shows on a shoestring budget when he was still a college student. "I had very grand fantasies of what I wanted to be and what that would mean," he said. While he knew he wanted to buy and sell art, he also understood that it could take years to become financially self-sufficient if he were to choose a career in a creative field. Still, when he graduated he began to raise money to fund his first larger-scale exhibition. Having watched his father fundraise in the financial industry over the years, he knew that what he was really asking was for people to invest and believe in him, as an individual. He wanted to live up to that belief in his potential.

For ten years, John lived off a fixed monthly check from his parents that had been calculated based on his rent and expenses when he graduated from college—"It was a ten-minute conversation," he said—and the amount of the check never increased over the years. "It wasn't always enough," he said, "and I really, desperately didn't ever want to ask for more."

While in some ways this subsidy could have fostered an unhealthy dependence, John had already sufficiently proved to his parents that he was serious and diligent in pursuing his efforts. His first gallery show got rave reviews. "It was challenging because my [shows] were 'successful,' but that doesn't mean I could take money and pay myself," he explained. "There was a dissonance between the appearance of success and the non-success financially. When that changed that was a very good thing."

Though he could not support himself at the beginning of his career, John understood that his parents recognized and appreciated his talents. They were able to assess his accomplishments because he consistently met and even exceeded independent standards of success: securing funding from people other than his parents, attracting ever-growing audiences to his viewings, consistently selling his artists' work, and revealing a consistent drive that led him to take on increasingly challenging projects.

"I'm really clear about how my father measures success," John said, "and nothing makes me happier now than my father knowing that I'm financially successful." While the goal was always financial independence, the journey toward achieving that was handled in such a way that no one was left scarred or bitter.

While it was difficult emotionally for this inheritor to accept support from his parents into his 30's, he also understood viscerally that this support was a gift without which he would not have been able to realize those grand dreams that had driven him for so long. "That ability to come to the city and explore different creative lives really requires support—that [creative] life is not conducive to rent paying . . . until it is," John said. "Money is not an arbiter of talent. My experience was the ideal scenario of making a creative life. A lot of people don't make it because the day job eats up the passion job."

The important message for parents to hear in this regard is that their children's *passion* for an activity has to be sustained and turned into something productive in order to be worth underwriting financially.

It takes patience (and hard work!) to find your "passion"

While many of our interviewees heard the message from their parents that finding a calling is secondary to getting on with being independent, others heard more nuanced messages, the most important of which is that passion isn't magical and that hard work—regardless of what kind of work—pays off.

David, the young man from San Francisco who worked as a dishwasher during one summer, was told by his mother: "Find something you're really passionate about, because when you're doing the work, it won't feel like work," but this was tempered with being told that this effort could take time. "It might not happen overnight; you might have to do the daily grind before you find your calling," she said. "Use this time to learn something and to keep your eyes open."

As a result, David, who is now in his mid-30's, feels comfortable working without quite having figured out yet if the position he occupies as an educational consultant is actually the perfect spot for him. "I know I probably haven't found my true calling," he says, "but through different experiences you have, something can trigger something else and maybe that will clue you in." In the meantime, he supports himself rather than waiting around for his true calling to come knocking on his door.

Susan, David's younger sister, heard the same message and used it as a kind of mantra to keep her going through rough patches when she questioned whether she would ever find what she really wanted to do. After college, she moved to Providence and started looking for a "real" job. "My checks started bouncing and I got a job working in a mailroom, stamping packages and doing shipping labels. But I just needed to be working," she said. Instead of feeling the job was demeaning, she just got on with it. In particular she remembers that her father never made her feel bad for "doing these crappy jobs. It was never 'my daughter is too good for this.'" He was happy that she was doing whatever was needed to do to stay employed and pay her own bills. Every work experience was seen as a rung on the ladder toward eventually finding the kind of sustainable work that she would enjoy. "You can learn from any job and you never know how it will work out or where it will lead."

In her job as a junior publishing executive, Sam—the young woman from Texas—found a way to combine her love of literature with her interest in business. It took some ingenuity to find a job in her field, and her expectations were in line with reality because her parents had helped her form those expectations. "I knew that you have to start at the bottom. You can't just go straight into your dream job," she said. "My dad always told me, you just need to keep working at it and it will pay off. To get to that point you have to work hard and go through obstacles."

Establish clear limits

Some people are called to a vocation early on in life, as Taylor was. As a teenager, she volunteered at Emory University Hospital in Atlanta, Georgia, on the weekends, playing with disabled children. She said that when it came time to find employment after college, "My parents told me I needed to engage in doing something meaningful—the purpose wasn't necessarily making money."

Soon Taylor realized that she wanted to attend medical school, an endeavor that would take a minimum of six years. During a discussion with her parents about what they would and would not pay for, they talked about rent. They said, "He who has a job can have his own apartment." Her parents made it clear that they didn't want to pay for her to have fun with friends; if going back to school was about studying for a career in medicine, then their philosophy was that it would be easiest for her to focus on this goal if she lived at home.

Many of our interviewees had similar experiences to Taylor's; their parents continued to give modest financial support after college, but did so within clear boundaries. The messages the children heard were about appreciation and dedication: If you wish to pursue this effort, we'd like you to prove your seriousness of purpose. An additional subtext was: *We are not a bottomless pit of funds.*

For two years Taylor lived in her childhood bedroom again while taking premed classes, before moving on to medical school. Once there, she was given money for both tuition and living expenses, but had to write out a budget for her father each semester. "They wanted me to be cognizant of where the money was going," she explained. Once she had a paying job as an internist, her parents helped her with a down payment on her first apartment without funding it outright. As a consequence, it is a significant responsibility for her to manage her mortgage on her own income. But she values the control she has over her purse strings.

Earlier in the book we met Daniel, the avid reader originally from Boston. When he decided to pursue a Ph.D. in history, his parents were supportive of his academic pursuits and set up expectations around finances and timing. They wanted to encourage his studies without falling into the common trap of underwriting years of unlimited and unpaid academic pursuits. "You can take all the time in the world to finish," they told him, "but we'll help you out for five years." In this way, they gave him the freedom to commit himself to his education to the extent that he felt was necessary, while giving themselves the freedom to eventually decrease financial support without derailing their son or causing unnecessary tension.

It is often exceptionally hard for parents in this situation to disentangle themselves from endlessly financing a young adult's studies. While there is goodwill at the onset, relations can become strained over time. Daniel's parents came up with an elegant solution that allowed them to be supportive, but within clear parameters.

Figuring out where to draw the line

When young adults spend their parents' money to support their daily lives rather than using money they've earned independently, this frequently creates an unhealthy and overly sensitive relationship to money overall. John, the gallery owner, explained that in his teens he became aware that he had the ability to buy whatever he wanted, "but I actually had no money. The money wasn't mine—the 'thing' was mine." Until he started to make "real" money from his exhibitions, he continued to have an uneasy relationship with money. "I never felt ownership of the capacity to buy until the money was *mine*."

This becomes unhealthy when children continue to feel conflicted and guilty about using their funds even in circumstances where that use is sanctioned and reasonable. Instead of making the most of the benefits of having access to money, they limit their spending and waste good opportunities. Sometimes they assuage their guilt about being dependent by becoming especially frugal, priding themselves on spending very little when in reality it is unnecessary—and may even inhibit them from making progress in their lives. Their vocational explorations become overly constrained and instead of launching, they are trapped by needlessly small-scale ambitions.

We often see parents eager to support their children's creative endeavors or business ideas without having a good grasp on how either they or their adult children should be defining success. Parents often unintentionally derail progress by trying to "help," for instance when they put money into a child's failing or fledgling business to keep it afloat—sometimes even when the child hasn't asked. Parents feel it's their responsibility to make the endeavor work simply because they have the money to help. If they don't step in, they feel like they are denying something vital to their child. Emotionally, it is nearly impossible for parents to sit back and do nothing; they invariably ask themselves, *what is the money for if not to help my child?*

Yet it is this very reluctance to help that kids often recall as among the most helpful things their parents did, because it forced the kids to be more self-reliant and resourceful. Matthew, the videographer, was given about $7,000 from his parents to launch his business, and his grandfather matched those funds. This totaled less than 25 percent of the start up cost. "They were always supportive," he explained, "but they never enabled me unless I was able to rally other support or do things myself." Although he knows he has a "soft pallet to fall back on" should things go wrong, he also said, "I've had to work for everything."

Likewise, Matteo's father invested in his first start-up, but gave him less than 10 percent of the total cost: "He invested at the same rate as everyone else. We never get preferential treatment," Matteo explained. He recounted the story of a wealthy friend whose business ended up tanking "because he was not given the tool kit to be and to remain independent," and he kept begging funds off his parents even when the venture was clearly failing.

When the cushion that breaks a fall is too thick and too soft, failing does not seem like such a terrible threat. But this is not actually the biggest problem. In this scenario, what undermines inheritors the most is how this cushion inhibits sound decision making. The lack of appropriate balance between confidence and caution will produce faulty logic, fueled alternately by insecurity or pride.

It became evident through our interviews that the best scenario for continuing to support a young person post college always included appropriate assessments of what they were truly able to accomplish on their own as well as constraints around the help so children understood that it was fixed. Sometimes that meant *not* injecting funds to keep a business or endeavor afloat or to help launch one.

The assessments must naturally be made on a case-by-case basis, but guardrails can be put up by setting up a defined time frame for support, or by judging success on the child's own terms. This usually involves seeing indications that the young person's efforts are valued and appreciated by others outside the family—as evidenced by the popularity of John's art gallery, for example, or the good reports from Daniel's thesis advisor.

When to say enough is enough

Parents are hardwired to help their children, whether by tying their shoes when they're toddlers, soothing hurt feelings in middle school, or helping smooth over the rough patches in early adulthood. There is nothing wrong with stepping in and giving your child a helping hand. What becomes destructive and under-mining—especially for children of means—is when parents insist on directing things from above like a benevolent deus ex machina providing constant, life-altering, godlike interventions.

Why is this behavior so damaging? It robs young people of their belief in their own capabilities. In Po Bronson and Ashley Merryman's book, *Top Dog*, they write about the healthy kind of striving that makes an individual perform well consistently and find good emotional balance in their lives. "Adaptive competi-tiveness is characterized by perseverance and determination to rise to the challenge, but it's bounded by an abiding respect for the rules," they write. "It's the ability to feel genuine satisfaction at having put in a worthy effort, even if you lose."[47]

In and of itself, lending a helping hand every now and then is not going to derail a child from developing his or her own capacity for adaptive competitiveness. But helping children born into affluence find the inner strength to make their way through life productively requires that parents set clear boundaries of support. And sometimes that means simply saying: *Enough is enough.*

How much *knowledge is power—and how much is destructive?*

Another issue wealthy parents wrestle with is how much to tell their children about the money and when. Our interviews revealed a fascinating and rather startling fact: Kids were better off when there was some uncertainty about *when* they would come into money and *how much* they would be getting.

In the debate about how much children should know about their family's wealth, there are many schools of thought, ranging along a spectrum from complete transparency to complete secrecy. Parents tend to feel more comfortable toward the secrecy end, worried that revealing too much about the money will rob their children of the motivation to succeed on their own terms. The wealth industry tends on the other hand to advocate transparency, with family meetings designed to educate children about the family's wealth, how it will intersect with their lives, and explain their future role in managing it (or giving it away).

Our interviews revealed that the optimal approach is in the middle, and that inheritors felt best launched into their own lives when the following was true:

- Their parents were honest about the fact that they had money.

- The children viewed the money as their parents' money that they worked hard for (and not as their own). Or, if the parents inherited it, the kids understood that the money belonged to a tradition of family wealth that existed before their parents and would carry on beyond their lives.

- The kids knew the money would eventually come to them but not when and not how much.

- In the meantime, the kids were free to design their own lives and be independently productive, not overly influenced by the family wealth or by the anticipation of their inheritance.

When uncertainty works

No doubt you've wondered: If I could find out whether I might get a disease one day, should I find out—or would I live a happier and more fruitful life if I were uncertain about the outcome? New research shows that, given the option, an astonishingly high number of people choose not to find out. Take, for instance, Huntington's disease, which is hereditary; anyone who has a parent with the disease stands a 50 percent chance of developing symptoms and dying. While a genetic test can now determine conclusively whether or not you have the marker for the disease, only five percent of those at risk take the test. So there was a benefit to the uncertainty that researchers had vastly underestimated. People who did not know were able to appreciate the present, focusing on the life they lived now.[48] It was not so different for our inheritors.

Earlier, we met Jane, originally from a farm in South Carolina. Now in her mid-20's and a high school teacher, Jane looks back on her financial education and believes that in many ways it was the *not knowing* with certainty how much money her parents had, and how much was coming her way, that enabled her to develop a sense of independence earlier. "It's beneficial that I didn't know about the trust," she said. "Knowing that your parents are wealthy is one thing. But knowing on top of that you have money available to you can change the decisions you make. If you know the money is there to fall back on, what's the incentive to work and to try harder? The money can allow you just to move on and not have to weather whatever is too hard."

Jane described the experiences of a childhood friend of her sister's who grew up with wealth. She continues to take college classes but keeps failing out, and her parents allow her to fail by continuing to support her disastrous academic efforts. "For example, if you know that you don't have to work because they'll just pay your bill," she said, "then it's more fun to sleep in [and not work]. But if you go down a path and you don't have money behind you, then you have to really dig in and stick it out."

Yet at the same time, Jane appreciates luxuries she gets to enjoy along with her parents. They take her skiing in their private plane and have helped her with her security deposit for her New York apartment. "I think if my dad had said to me as I went off to college that I had money, I don't know how that would have worked out."

Similarly, Peter—the writer who lives in L.A.—now knows that he will most likely inherit a large sum of money, though he still doesn't know exactly how much, and he *likes* not knowing. "I don't have any confidence that the money I'll inherit will cover the lifestyle I want and that uncertainty is very helpful. I think to myself I will need to make *some* money from writing and I will need to sell a film in order to support my lifestyle, and that fear is very motivating."

Each day, he forces himself back to his desk to overcome the doubt about whether his screenplays will sell. Like many creatives, he loves his work, but the lure of distractions and his insecurities always threaten to pull him away. "There are people who have an inner drive and that's all they need, and so that kid, if he has a couple of million waiting for him, that's not really going to have an effect on whether or not he's going to be successful in his professional life," Peter explained. "But then there are a lot of kids who don't have that drive and need the extra push." He counts himself among the latter group.

Timing matters

Currently, the wealth advising industry proposes that great wealth should be seen as "family money" and that children should be involved early on in understanding it and managing it. They should appreciate what the money is used for and why, and should play an active role in the family's philanthropic efforts. As we discussed earlier in this book, far less attention is paid to the critical developmental stage that allows children to separate from their families and become their own person, not overly influenced by the money. These stories speak loud and clear about how important it is for parents not to disrupt this critical developmental stage. For young adults wrestling with identity formation, career development, and separation from the family, a focus on the family wealth and its role in their lives can be distracting at best or disruptive at worst. Wealthy parents should focus during this period on doing what they can to support their children in developing the success factors we identified earlier in chapter 1 (see page 23). Being granted a reprieve from the influence of family wealth on their lives allows children to develop these traits more quickly. There is a time and place for the children of wealthy parents to learn more about the responsibilities and rewards of their inheritance, but the time should be after they have developed the four success factors, not before.

Parting Thoughts

....

It truly was a joy to have the opportunity to learn from each of these individuals and then in turn to share their stories and hard-won lessons with others. All too often, money saps young adults of their energy and turns them into cynics. Yet the inheritors we spoke with embraced life—its downs as well as its ups—with vigor, determination, confidence, and optimism. Let their stories be an inspiration and support to you as you make the hard decisions involved every day in parenting. On behalf of all who will be inspired by their words, I thank them.

And thank you again to all of my colleagues and partners who supported the development of this project. While the firm covered the costs of publication and enabled me to dedicate a portion of my time to this effort, this work represents my opinions and does not necessarily represent the opinions of the firm. I was gratefully given complete editorial autonomy, and therefore any errors are my own.

Tools and Resources

A Thank You from Successful Inheritors to Their Parents:
A Summary of the Key Messages for Raising Grounded and Successful Children of Wealth

....

- Although we might have complained at the time, when we got older we were grateful that you set limits, held us accountable, and had high expectations of our behavior.

- Although we might have asked you to do more to help us at the time, looking back we realize the most helpful thing you did was show us that you knew we could do it on our own. You were right.

- Although there were times when we struggled that were really painful for you to watch, what we take most from those experiences is the pride in ourselves that we made it through. And we know we will be able to make it through when we encounter other difficulties in our lives.

- We are grateful that you taught us sound money values by living them in your own lives. Watching you, we came to understand that material possessions don't make a life, people and character are more important than money, and that just because we have it doesn't mean that we have to spend it.

- The family stories you told us helped us understand that our family didn't always have this money, we easily might not have it again, and in the meantime we should be focused in our own lives on making sure we will be able to thrive in either circumstance.

- Because you asked us to, we learned how to keep track of and be accountable for the money we were spending.

- By emphasizing how appreciative we should be for the things we had, you helped us develop a sense of gratitude for the opportunities you provided us in life.

- Thank you, thank you, thank you for requiring us to work—in the home, outside the home, in high school and out of college. You have given us gifts that are worth more than any money we could inherit: an internally sustaining purpose and motivation in life and an understanding of the world outside the wealth we've known.

- Your advice that every job is worthwhile and that you can learn from every experience really helped us stick it out in those first couple of work years. We're so glad we did because those tough experiences lead to the work we now love.

- You showed us through your own behavior that work is about more than money—it's about contribution, purpose, pride, and satisfaction.

- Your expecting us to try to support ourselves out of college was key to our happiness. We feel best about ourselves when we are able to cover most of the costs of our own lifestyle.

- It's been so important in our lives for us to be able show people that we can make it on our own—that we earned our success and that it's not just the result of our parents' influence or affluence. Thank you for giving us the chance to prove that to ourselves and to the world.

Afterword

....

I am grateful to my friend and colleague Coventry Edwards-Pitt ("Covie") for writing this important work. It brings a clarity to parents of means that has long been lacking.

In my capacity as president of Ballentine Partners, LLC, I understand keenly how wealth can complicate parenting. Almost a decade ago, my partners and I saw patterns in the wealthy community that were unsettling. Why were so many children of affluence struggling? It wasn't all of them, but it was apparent that serious issues were present far too frequently in these families. And it was our feeling that they should be happening less than in the population at large; after all, these families have the financial resources to afford whatever they would need to address these issues. These were not lazy, inattentive, or entitled parents. To the contrary, most of them were highly successful, driven people.

When we shared our observations with other professionals in the community serving wealthy families, it garnered nearly universal acknowledgment. Hundreds of professionals over the course of a few years nodded their heads in vigorous agreement that the problems were real and epidemic. But few seemed to be asking many of the potentially important questions, and answers were even more elusive. We began bringing in Dr. Jim Grubman to convene regular discussions among our staff so that we could be better prepared to help families manage the difficult issues they were facing with their children.

Throughout these years, Covie has shown exceptional skill and passion in this area. When she became chief wealth advisory officer of our firm two years ago, she was intent on using her position of thought leadership to try to better understand and potentially solve the conundrum of how parents can avoid these problems to raise children who are happy, independent, and motivated.

She soon saw the need for this book; a book dedicated to interviewing children who were successful in order to learn from them what they thought accounted for their success. As we knew our clients would benefit from the results, we were happy to support Covie by enabling her to allocate her time to the book and supporting the costs of production. At the same time, we have given Covie complete authorial and editorial autonomy in this project.

The book reveals fascinating truths for families of wealth to consider when raising their children. That the value of working, and learning what it means to work for others, has powerful formative repercussions later in life. These children learn what it means to have someone expect something of them, be accountable for the results of their efforts, have someone thank them for their work, and develop a productive role in the world. Covie brings to light the importance of experiencing scarcity, even if just for a short time. The children who do learn not to fear it; consequently, they are freer to enjoy rather than feel dependent on their wealth. And she illustrates for readers how formative the post-college years can be. It is a time that we used to think of as "adulthood achieved, parenting mission accomplished!" In reality, it's just the time our children are learning to establish their places within the world. To find them, they have to take risks and truly launch.

The paradox of this book is that the children of wealth who feel most successful are less likely to actually need the family wealth. What role, then, does it play in their lives? I have worked with many wealthy parents thinking over this exact question. Successful families, however, do not see this as some sort of tragic irony, as though the money itself were seeking purpose. Because it turns out that healthy, wealthy, and wise adults can help their parents make better decisions about family legacy and stewardship. Whether the choices they make involve keeping it for security, giving it to charity, or deploying it to their own industry, these parents can take pride in seeing the family's resources contribute to the very striving, and thriving, that they always hoped for.

Drew McMorrow
President, Ballentine Partners

Recommended Reading

Ginsburg, Kenneth R. *Building Resilience in Children and Teens: Giving Kids Roots and Wings.* Elk Grove Village, IL: American Academy of Pediatrics. 2011.

Godfrey, Joline. *Raising Financially Fit Kids.* New York: Ten Speed Press. 2003, 2013.

Hausner, Lee. *Children of Paradise: Successful Parenting for Prosperous Families.* New York: Penguin Group. 1990, 2005.

Hughes, James E. Jr., Susan Massenzio, and Keith Whitaker. *The Cycle of the Gift: Family Wealth and Wisdom.* Hoboken, NJ: Bloomberg Press. 2012.

Kindlon, Dan. *Too Much of a Good Thing: Raising Children of Character in an Indulgent Age.* New York: Miramax. 2001.

Levine, Madeline. *The Price of Privilege: How Parental Pressure and Material Advantage Are Creating a Generation of Disconnected and Unhappy Kids.* New York: HarperCollins. 2006.

Levine, Mel. *Ready or Not, Here Life Comes*. New York: Simon & Shuster. 2006.

Levy, John L. *Inherited Wealth: Opportunities and Dilemmas*. Charleston, SC: BookSurge Publishing. 2008.

Mogel, Wendy. *The Blessing of a Skinned Knee: Using Jewish Teachings to Raise Self-Reliant Children*. New York: Scribner. 2008.

Morris, Richard A. and Jayne A. Pearl. *Kids, Wealth, and Consequences: Ensuring a Responsible Financial Future for the Next Generation*. Hoboken, NJ: Bloomberg Press. 2010.

Perry, Ellen Miley. *A Wealth of Possibilities: Navigating Family, Money, and Legacy*. Washington, DC: Egremont Press. 2012.

Salzer, Myra. *The Inheritor's Sherpa: A Life-Summiting Guide for Inheritors*. Boulder: Wealth Conservancy. 2005.

Schwartz, Barry. *The Paradox of Choice: Why More Is Less*. New York: Harper Perennial. 2005.

Stovall, Jim. *The Ultimate Gift*. Colorado Springs: David C. Cook. 2007.

Taylor, James. *Positive Pushing: How to Raise a Successful and Happy Child*. New York: Hyperion. 2003.

Tough, Paul. *How Children Succeed: Grit, Curiosity, and the Hidden Power of Character*. New York: Mariner Books. 2013.

Notes

....

Introduction

[1] Malcolm Gladwell, *David and Goliath: Underdogs, Misfits, and the Art of Battling Giants* (New York: Little, Brown and Company, 2013), 44–52.

Chapter One

[2] Viktor E. Frankl, *Man's Search for Meaning* (New York: Simon & Schuster, 1963), 166.

[3] Carol S. Dweck, *Mindset: The New Psychology of Success* (New York: Ballentine Books, 2006), 21.

[4] Ibid, 41.

[5] Jay Hughes, *Family: The Compact Among Generations* (New York: Bloomberg Press, 2007).

[6] Angela L. Duckworth, Christopher Peterson, Michael D. Matthews, and Dennis R. Kelly, "Grit: Perseverance and Passion for Long-Term Goals,"
http://www.sas.upenn.edu/~duckwort/images/Grit%20JPSP.pdf.

[7] Robert Biswas-Diener and Todd B. Kashdan, *Psychology Today*, July

2, 2013, http://www.psychologytoday.com/articles/201306/what-happy-people-do-differently?tr=MostViewed.

[8] James Taylor. *Positive Pushing* (New York: Hyperion, 2002), 247.

Chapter Two

[9] Dweck, *Mindset,* 211, 173.

[10] Lori Gottleib, "How to Land Your Kid in Therapy," *The Atlantic,* June 7, 2011, http://www.theatlantic.com/magazine/archive/2011/07/how-to-land-your-kid-in-therapy/308555/.

[11] Ibid.

[12] Madeline Levine, *The Price of Privilege* (New York: HarperCollins, 2006), 17.

[13] Lee Hausner, *Children of Paradise* (Irvine, CA: Plaza Press, 2005), 242.

[14] Ibid.

[15] Barry Schwartz, *The Paradox of Choice* (New York: Harper Perennial, 2005), 99.

[16] Wendy Mogel, *The Blessing of a Skinned Knee* (New York: Simon & Shuster, 2001), 91.

[17] Ibid.

[18] Brad Klontz, Rick Kahler, and Ted Klontz, *Facilitating Financial Health* (Cincinnati: National Underwriter Company, 2008), 127.

[19] Levine, *The Price of Privilege*, 17.

[20] Dan Kindlon, *Too Much of a Good Thing,* http://www.dankindlon.com/too-much/.

[21] Ellen Miley Perry, *A Wealth of Possibilities* (Washington, DC: Egremont Press, 2012), 43, 71, 73.

[22] Taylor, *Positive Pushing*, xvii, 3.

[23] Ibid.

[24] Myra Salzer, *The Inheritor's Sherpa* (Boulder, CO: Wealth Conservancy, 2005), 45.

[25] Taylor, *Positive Pushing.* xvii, 3.

[26] Levine, *The Price of Privilege*, 17.

Chapter Three

[27] Lewis Mandell and Linda Schmid Klein, "The Impact of Financial Literacy Education on Subsequent Financial Behavior," *Journal of Financial Counseling and Planning* 20, no. 1, (2009).

[28] Jennifer G. Bohanek et al., "Family Narrative Interaction and Children's Sense of Self," *Family Process* 45, no. 1 (2006), http://www.psychology.emory.edu/cognition/fivush/lab/FivushLabWebsite/papers/FamilyNarrativeandInteraction.pdf.

[29] Ibid.

Chapter Four

[30] Paul Tough, *How Children Succeed: Grit, Curiosity and the Hidden Power of Character* (New York: Mariner Books, 2013).

[31] Mihaly Csikszentmihalyi, *If We Are So Rich, Why Aren't We Happy?,* *American Psychologist* 54, no. 10 (October 1999).

[32] Larry Stylbel interview, RIABiz, September 18, 2013, http://www.riabiz.com/a/24082002/a-quick-take-from-a-harvard-psychologist-on-how-the-obscenely-rich-can-think-about-passing-on-a-work-ethic.

[33] Martin Seligman, *Flourish* (New York: Atria, New York, 2012).

[34] "Number of Jobs Held, Labor Market Activity, and Earnings Growth among the Youngest Baby Boomers," Bureau of Labor Statistics news release, July 25, 2012, http://www.bls.gov/news.release/pdf/nlsoy.pdf.

[35] Jeanne Meister, "Three Ways to Prevent a Human Resource Nightmare," WOBI, September, 2012, http://www.wobi.com/blog/generations/three-ways-prevent-human-resource-nightmare.

[36] Camilla Tominy, "Queen's Devotion to Duty Helped Shape His Working Life," *Express,* June 2, 2013,
http://www.express.co.uk/news/royal/404351/
Peter-Phillips-tells-how-the-Queen-s-devotion-to-duty-helped-to-shape-his-working-life.

Chapter Five

[37] Paul Tough, *How Children Succeed*, 84.

[38] John L. Levy, *Inherited Wealth* (Charleston, SC: BookSurge Publishing, 2008), 19, 21.

[39] http://www.selfdeterminationtheory.org/browse-publications/index
.php?option=com_sdt&view=SearchPublications&task=domain-Search&domain=11.

[40] Jessica Pressler, "Hammer Time," *Elle*, June 20, 2013.

[41] Fredda Herz Brown and Dennis T. Jaffe, "Overcoming Entitlement and Raising Responsible Next Generation Family Members," Relative Solutions. 2010.

Chapter Six

[42] Cal Newport, "Solving Gen Y's Passion Problem," September 18, 2012, http://blogs.hbr.org/2012/09/solving-gen-ys-passion-problem/.

[43] Ibid.

[44] Oliver Segovia, "To Find Happiness, Forget About Passion," January 13, 2012, http://blogs.hbr.org/2012/01/to-find-happiness-forget-about/.

[45] Ibid.

[46] Mel Levine, *Ready or Not, Here Life Comes* (New York: Simon & Shuster, 2005), 87.

[47] Po Bronson and Ashley Merryman, *Top Dog: The Science of Winning and Losing* (New York: Twelve Books, 2013), 11.

[48] "Do You Really Want to Know Your Future?" Freakonomics radio podcast, June 20, 2013, http://freakonomics.com/2013/06/20/do-you-really-want-to-know-your-future-full-transcript/.

Notes

Notes

Notes

Notes

Notes